PAY ATTENTION

How Paying Attention Can Help You Live Your Best Life

ROGER GRIST

TRILOGY
PROFESSIONAL PUBLISHING MEETS POWERFUL PROMOTION
A wholly owned subsidiary of TBN

Trilogy Christian Publishers

A Wholly Owned Subsidiary of Trinity Broadcasting Network

2442 Michelle Drive

Tustin, CA 92780

Copyright © 2023 by Roger Grist

All Scripture quotations, unless otherwise noted, taken from THE HOLY BIBLE, NEW INTERNATIONAL VERSION®, NIV® Copyright © 1973, 1978, 1984, 2011 by Biblica, Inc.® Used by permission. All rights reserved worldwide.

Scripture quotations marked BSB are taken from The Holy Bible, Berean Standard Bible, BSB. Copyright ©2016, 2020, 2022 by Bible Hub. Used by Permission. All Rights Reserved Worldwide.

Scripture quotations marked NKJV are taken from the New King James Version®. Copyright © 1982 by Thomas Nelson. Used by permission. All rights reserved.

All rights reserved, including the right to reproduce this book or portions thereof in any form whatsoever.

For information, address Trilogy Christian Publishing

Rights Department, 2442 Michelle Drive, Tustin, Ca 92780.

Trilogy Christian Publishing/ TBN and colophon are trademarks of Trinity Broadcasting Network.

For information about special discounts for bulk purchases, please contact Trilogy Christian Publishing.

Manufactured in the United States of America

Trilogy Disclaimer: The views and content expressed in this book are those of the author and may not necessarily reflect the views and doctrine of Trilogy Christian Publishing or the Trinity Broadcasting Network.

10 9 8 7 6 5 4 3 2 1

Library of Congress Cataloging-in-Publication Data is available.

ISBN 979-8-88738-754-3

ISBN 979-8-88738-755-0 (ebook)

DEDICATION

I want to dedicate this book to my Lord and Savior, Jesus Christ, who saved me, set me free, and has given me His Spirit of love, power, and a sound mind.

ACKNOWLEDGMENT

I want to thank my wife, Nancy, and our daughters, Alexandra and Elizabeth, for supporting me during the past many years of ordained ministry and work on this book. Their love and support helped me at each step along this journey.

I want to thank my church family, St. Anne's Anglican Church in Fort Worth, TX, for their encouragement and love, helping me to learn many of the things in this book.

Thanks go out to all my fellow Christians and church members in my various churches who taught me many things that helped mold this book.

TABLE OF CONTENTS

Introduction..................................... 9

Pay Attention to Your Body 11

Pay Attention to Your Mind and Emotions.......... 29

Pay Attention to Your Spiritual Life 35

Pay Attention to the Voice of God 99

Pay Attention to Your Family 139

Pay Attention to Your Church................... 157

Conclusion.................................... 179

About the Author 181

Bibliography 183

INTRODUCTION

"Roger, would you pay attention?" My mother would often say this as she tried to tell me something of great importance. I would either be daydreaming or focusing on the latest cartoon on television.

I caused my mother no end of frustration as she would try to communicate something to me. This usually resulted in her yelling at me or in some sort of punishment.

As I look at my life, I realize there are many times I fail to pay attention to the things around me, sometimes important things.

There are things pertaining to my physical life that have sometimes sought my attention. Often those things were ignored. There were incidences in the past when I did not pay attention to aspects of my emotional life, causing undue worry or unhealthy habits.

The spiritual life is probably one of the most neglected areas in the lives of busy people today. I have failed, from time to time, to pay attention to my spiritual life.

This failure has affected not only my relationship with God but also the physical and emotional parts of my life.

Our physical and spiritual lives can also be affected by our emotional lives. How do we handle our emotions? Are there events in the past that continue to haunt us or have a subconscious effect on us and our relationships?

I have included many passages of Scripture because, in the end, it is not my words that will have any lasting effect upon the reader but the Word of God. As the writer of Hebrews puts it, "For the word of God is alive and active. Sharper than any double-edge sword, it pierces even to dividing soul and spirit, joints and marrow; it judges the thoughts and attitudes of the heart" (Hebrews 4:12).

In other words, God's Word written and Jesus Christ (the Word incarnate) can change our thoughts and actions. I encourage you to pay attention to the word of God throughout this work.

During the course of this book you will begin to see how many things either bring good or ill to our lives based on how well we pay attention.

This book may not transform your life. It will, however, cause you to become more aware of the things in your life which, if you focus on them, are aware of them, and don't simply flit past them, will make your life more effective, more efficient, and more enjoyable.

All of this will be accomplished as you learn to *Pay Attention*.

PAY ATTENTION TO YOUR BODY

One of the things we are prone to do as human beings is buy into the philosophy that if you ignore it, it will go away or if you don't pay attention to it, nothing will happen.

When it comes to our bodies, we must pay attention. God says in Scripture that we are "fearfully and wonderfully made"(Psalm 139:14).

Before we can pay attention to our bodies, we must look at something which could very well affect not just our bodies but our whole being.

Although we are made in the image of God and we are fearfully and wonderfully made, we have a problem. That problem is sin.

When God created each aspect of His creation, He pronounced it good (Genesis 1). This included man and woman as a part of the good creation.

God gave the first humans complete freedom within this good creation. However, while God gave them many permissions, such as, "You are free to eat from any tree in the garden" (Genesis 2:16). He did give them a prohibition, "but you must not eat from the tree of the knowledge of good and evil, for when you eat from it you will certainly die" (Genesis 2:17).

We read in Genesis 3 that Satan came along in the form of a serpent and sought to place doubt in the mind of Eve when he said, "Did God really say, 'You must not eat from ANY tree in the garden'?" (Genesis 3:1).

You notice that Satan twisted God's word making it say something that God did not say. We see many examples of that in our modern world when people question the Word of God, the Bible. They seek to make God say something He never said or intended to say.

Satan's main goal today is to get people to question everything in the Bible that goes against the prevailing philosophies in secular societies.

When Eve and Adam ate of the forbidden fruit, something happened to them. Death entered into their lives. First spiritual death, and then physical death. Before this fall of man the Bible seems to indicate that man was meant to live eternally.

Listen to how Paul puts it in Romans 5:12, "Therefore, just as sin entered the world through one man, and death through sin, and in this way death came to all people, because all sinned."

So, sin became a form of genetic disease that is passed on to each human being. Because sin entered the world the whole creation was also affected.

PAY ATTENTION TO YOUR BODY

> I consider that our present sufferings are not worth comparing with the glory that will be revealed in us. For the creation waits in eager expectation for the children of God to be revealed. For the creation was subjected to frustration, not by its own choice, but by the will of the one who subjected it, in hope that the creation itself will be liberated from its bondage to decay and brought into the freedom and glory of the children of God.
> **Romans 8:18–21**

The whole creation was affected by sin. Could this be the reason why we have earthquakes, tornados, hurricanes, droughts, and floods? It shouldn't surprise us that we seem to see an increase in these things occurring. The Bible says that these things will increase as the day of the Lord draws closer (Matthew 24).

The evidence also points to sin having affected human life with the human body breaking down, diseases previously unknown now being manifest, unusual birth defects, etc.

Moses writes that before man and woman were created, God said,

> Let us make mankind in our image, in our likeness, so that they may rule over the fish in the sea and the birds of the sky, over the livestock and all the wild animals, and over all the creatures that move along the ground.
> **Genesis 1:26**

PAY ATTENTION

Many have suggested that the "us" and "our" in this passage is referring to the members of the Trinity speaking to one another about the creation of mankind.

If human beings were created in the image of God, then what does that mean? Jesus answers that question when He said in John 4:24 "God is spirit." God's nature or essence is spiritual, thus, we (as His creation) are spiritual in essence or nature. God is not a giant man sitting on a throne with a white beard and glowing eyes. The Bible uses imagery like this to help us to better apprehend the role of God ruling over His creation. We cannot fully comprehend the fullness of God or God's nature.

When God created Adam in Genesis 2:7, He breathed into Adam the breath of life. The word breath in Hebrew means spirit. So, Adam was created with a human spirit. That human spirit was designed to have a relationship with the God who is spirit, and in whose image man and woman are made.

As a result of the sin of Adam and Eve, sin corrupted their human spirits and they no longer enjoyed the relationship they were originally created to have with their Creator.

Each human being who came into the world after them had spirits that were corrupted with a sinful nature. They were not able to have an unbroken relationship with God.

PAY ATTENTION TO YOUR BODY

From Genesis 3, God put in place a plan to redeem our sinful human natures by bringing into the world someone who had come from God's presence. "And I will put enmity between you and the woman, and between your offspring and hers; he will crush your head, and you will strike his heel" (Genesis 3:15).

The offspring to which Genesis 3 refers is Jesus. Satan would, figuratively speaking, strike Christ's heel at the crucifixion, but Jesus would ultimately crush Satan through His resurrection. He became victorious over the devil and his works (1 John 3:8).

Satan was an angel created by God to worship the Almighty. However, Satan rebelled against God and was cast down to earth (Revelation 12:9). The devil or Satan is described by Jesus in the Bible as one who has come to this earth to "steal and kill and destroy" (John 10:10). He is described as "a roaring lion looking for someone to devour" (1 Peter 5:8). His goal is to try to steal every soul away from a commitment to God and make that soul dedicated to him (Satan) and his kingdom.

That plan was thwarted when the Father sent His Son (the Word of God) to the earth being conceived by the Holy Spirit and born in the womb of the Virgin Mary. God prophesied through Isaiah that He would do this, "Therefore, the Lord himself will give you a sign: The virgin will

PAY ATTENTION

conceive and give birth to a son and will call him Immanuel" (Isaiah 7:14). According to Matthew, Immanuel means "God with us" (Matthew 1:23).

Once the Word of God came to this earth He became "flesh and dwelt among us" (John 1:14, NKJV). He was then given a "name that is above every name" (Philippians 2:9).

This child, conceived in the womb of the Virgin Mary by the Holy Spirit, would be named Jesus and grow up to become the Savior of the world (Matthew 1:20–21). Around the age of thirty, this child, now a man, would live the perfect life the moral law of God required and be accepted as the perfect sacrifice for the sins of the whole world.

When Jesus died on the cross, was buried, and rose from the dead on the third day (as He predicted He would), He fulfilled what the prophets had predicted about the coming the Messiah, the Savior.

The third chapter of John's Gospel is very revealing about the plan of God for all people. Jesus says no less than three times "Very, truly" which is God's way of saying *pay attention* to what I am about to say. Jesus goes on to describe to Nicodemus God's plan of salvation.

As the world's savior, Jesus said that all people need to be "born again" of the Spirit (John 3:3). In other words, their sinful natures or human spirits infected with sin, need

PAY ATTENTION TO YOUR BODY

to be transformed and made right before God. Jesus said that a person is born again when that person receives Jesus as their Savior. When they receive Him, the Holy Spirit comes to live inside of them (John 14:17). They are born of God and are children of God (John 1:12–13).

When the Holy Spirit comes to mingle with our human spirit (Romans 8:16), we now have a relationship with God that humans were originally designed to have. We become children of God and we have fellowship and access to God through the Spirit (Ephesians 2:18).

Even though we are made right with God by virtue of being born again, our spirits and our bodies are still not fully redeemed. That redemption will not happen until Christ comes back again to usher in His new creation to replace this old dying creation (Isaiah 65:17–19; 2 Peter 3:13; Revelation 21:1).

Because our bodies are still subject to the decay brought on by sin, those bodies have to deal with pain, disease, breakdown, and illness. The good news is that there is a God who heals. "who forgives all your sins and heals all your diseases" (Psalm 103:3).

Could it be that our bodies are speaking to us? If that is the case, how often do we ignore our bodies and pretend that they are not speaking to us?

Part of this willingness to ignore our bodies comes

from those who are extreme in the opposite way. They hear their bodies telling them all sorts of things that just are not true. These people are often described as hypochondriacs. They would be the sort of folks that want these words engraved on their tombstones, "I told you I was sick."

We don't want to be like those people who are always complaining to us about their physical woes. We think by ignoring the voice of our bodies, we can believe that we are really protecting ourselves from being perceived as neurotic.

We also don't want to be like those who call the doctor at every little sniffle or sneeze. I have known of a person who had their doctor's number on speed dial, they called their physician so often.

How can we find the right balance of listening to our bodies and not being hyper-sensitive to every little ache or pain?

The answer is not an exact science. We learn to listen to our bodies by trial and error. I remember one time I had a headache. I felt like my body was saying, "you have a brain tumor." After consulting a medical website, and taking an over the counter medicine, my headache went away. I concluded I did not have a brain tumor.

I have since started trying to listen to my body more closely. I can now tell that when I have a headache, which

PAY ATTENTION TO YOUR BODY

I rarely have, it is probably something caused by stress, overexertion, or withdrawal from caffeine in my tea or Dr. Pepper which I used to regularly drink. I believe I at one time kept the Dr. Pepper company afloat.

I trust that I will be able to recognize when a headache is more than a normal physical ailment. There may, indeed, be times when I might need to contact a physician and have tests run.

Whatever my thoughts on my physical condition, I must heed the words of the scripture found in 2 Chronicles 16:12: "In the thirty-ninth year of his reign Asa was afflicted with a disease in his feet. Though his disease was severe, even in his illness he did not seek help from the Lord, but only from the physicians."

Often when my body speaks to me, I don't immediately seek guidance or even healing from the Lord. Physicians can be helpful in diagnosing what is going on in your body. They are not God, and thus, they may not always know what is wrong or how best to treat it.

There are times when the physical symptoms we have in our bodies may reflect what is going on in our minds or in our spirits.

It should be no surprise that there is a connection between our bodies, minds and spirits. After all, we are made in the image of God, a reflection of the Trinitarian nature of God (in the essence of the one God, there are three persons – the Father, the Son and the Holy Spirit). Even though God is one (Deuteronomy 6:4) and God is spirit (John 4:24), there are three parts to God's oneness. Even though the essence of who we are is spirit, we, too have three parts that make us human (spirit, soul and body).

One of the Eucharistic prayers from the Episcopal Book of Common Prayer makes this statement "From the primal elements you brought forth the human race and blessed us with memory, reason, and skill. You made us the rulers of creation, but we turned against you and we turned against one another" (Episcopal Church 1875, 370).

What the Bible and that prayer are describing are the intricacies of the human creation. We were created physically with a body of flesh, blood, and bones. That physical body was created for a specific purpose: to house the other two unique aspects of God's amazing design, the mind (soul) and the spirit.

When God made man (Adam) physically He then imparted to him a mind. This mind reflects the mind of the Creator. It is a mind capable of remembering (memory), thinking logically with understanding (reason) and with the ability to reflect a small portion of the Creator's resourceful abilities to create new, beautiful, helpful, wonderful things to make human life better (skill).

PAY ATTENTION TO YOUR BODY

The mind is the vehicle through which the voice of the body speaking to us is processed. It is through the mind that we rationally interpret what the rest of the body is saying to us.

Obviously, the health of the mind can cause a misdiagnosis of the body's voice resulting in physical problems.

> A man is convinced he is dead. His wife and kids are exasperated. They keep telling him he's not dead. But he continues to insist he's dead. They try telling him, "Look, you're not dead; you're walking and talking and breathing; how can you be dead?" But he continues to insist he is dead. The family finally takes him to a doctor. The doctor pulls out some medical books to demonstrate to the man that dead men do not bleed. After some time, the man admits that dead men do not bleed. The doctor then takes the man's hand and a needle and pokes the end of his finger. The man starts bleeding. He looks at his finger and says, "What do you know? *Dead mean do bleed!*" (Zeolla, 1999)

The mind can play all sorts of tricks on a person convincing them of ailments that aren't really there, or conditions that don't exist. Sometimes the mind loses its ability to reason, to think rationally, and then we do not clearly hear what our bodies are trying to tell us.

PAY ATTENTION

The body often tries to convey to the mind that something is amiss and needs our attention. The journey of life is spent learning to accurately discern and pay attention to what the body is trying to say to the mind.

Many do not realize that the body and mind are meant to work in harmony for the common good of our lives.

Christians are told in Scripture that they have "the mind of Christ" (1 Corinthians 2:16). By this mind, the Christian can begin to have his thoughts come more in line with the thoughts of God. Also, the mind of Christ gives one the ability to think about and look at things from more than a human perspective.

If the things our minds think about are important to God, then it would make sense that God would want us to think with the mind of Christ.

If God speaks to us (and Scripture indicates He does), then God will reveal things that we need to know from the physical condition or symptoms of our bodies. He will also try to give reason, insight, knowledge, and discernment to our minds to help us adequately determine which course of action should be taken to address our physical condition.

God might speak to us that we need to seek out a physician to help us with our condition after we have first sought healing from the Lord. Not all physicians may be able to give us a proper diagnosis. Perhaps they have not paid attention to the latest medical developments or failed to pay attention to all that we are communicating.

PAY ATTENTION TO YOUR BODY

Students at the LSU Med School were receiving their first anatomy class with a real dead human body. They are all gathered around the surgery table with the body covered with a white sheet. Then the professor started the class by telling them: "In medicine, it is necessary to have two [sic] important qualities as a doctor: The first is that it is necessary that you not be disgusted." The Professor uncovered the sheet, sunk his finger in the butt of the dead body, withdrew it and sucked it. "Go ahead and do the same thing," he told his students. The students freaked out, hesitated and subsequently taking turns, stuck their finger in the butt of the dead body and sucked it after withdrawing it. When everyone finished, the Professor looked at them and told them: "The second important quality is observation. I stuck the middle finger and sucked the index finger. Pay attention people!" (Short, 2002).

Even doctors can be guilty of not paying attention to us and to our bodies, but instead, may just revert to what they have done in the past thinking that will suffice.

As I write this, our world is in the midst of a pandemic. COVID-19 has infected all parts of our world. Doctors and medical professionals all across the health care spectrum disagree about the transmissibility, effectiveness of mask wearing, treatment options, benefits of lockdowns and so on.

PAY ATTENTION

We have seen our liberties challenged and sometimes removed in the name of a multi-opinioned scientific community. We were told that if we wear a mask (or two or three) then we will soon be beyond this pandemic. Then we were told if we socially distance then that will bring this virus to its knees. Along comes a vaccine for the virus and we were told that if we get the vaccine we will be protected from the virus. Lo and behold, we find out that not only can a vaccinated person get the virus, they can transmit it to a healthy person and possibly die from it as well. Those who have contracted the virus and survived have been told they must still wear a mask and avoid large crowds. Even in countries that are fully vaccinated, the virus continues to spread.

Many are seeking to force or mandate vaccinations. Those who pay attention to their bodies and who may have concerns about receiving a currently unproven vaccine are called murderers because they may be infecting other unvaccinated, who have made the choice to take the risk of being infected.

Whom do we believe or pay attention to when it comes to advice given regarding our bodies?

We may not like to pay attention to our bodies because we might discover something we don't want to address.

PAY ATTENTION TO YOUR BODY

I remember gaining a lot of weight which mainly showed around my waist and stomach. I never like to look at myself in the mirror and didn't want to listen to God speak to me about my body. I would hear verses from Scripture like,

> Do you not know that your bodies are temples of the Holy Spirit, who is in you, whom you have received from God? You are not your own; you were bought with a price. Therefore, honor God with your bodies.
> **1 Corinthians 6:19–20**

I tried to justify my weight gain by saying that it doesn't matter what a person looks like on the outside. The Lord told Samuel to go to Jesse to pick one of his sons to be the next king of Israel. Samuel looked at Eliab and thought surely this is the one, he looks very kingly. But the Lord said to Samuel, "Do not consider his appearance or his height, for I have rejected him; the Lord does not look at things people look at. People look at the outward appearance, but the Lord looks at the heart" (1 Samuel 16:7).

While it is true that God does not judge us based on our outward appearance, God's design for our bodies is to seek to do what we can to be healthy. My stomach was not a reflection of good health. Even knowing this was not enough for me to pay attention to my health. I was not willing to change until a young child said to me during a Vacation Bible School at our church, "Are you pregnant?" She didn't say that because she was told in school that men can get pregnant. She looked at me and decided I was pregnant. I was humiliated enough to pay attention to my body and began to make changes that resulted in my losing some of that belly fat. This resulted in my feeling better physically and emotionally.

When I paid attention to my body I began to look at what I put in my body. As I mentioned before, I love Dr. Pepper. I used to be a Dr. Pepper addict. This was well known among my parishioners, who in the past would make sure that elixir was available at potlucks or special events.

One of the hardest things I had to give up was my DP. It was amazing what difference it made physically. I also began to reduce foods that were not so good for me, mainly fried foods and sugar-filled goodies.

I have not always been successful at paying attention to these things, sometimes resulting in reverting to my old eating habits. When I paid attention to the Lord speaking to me through my body, I began to see real changes.

How about you? What is your body saying to you? Could it be the Lord speaking to you about His temple?

I've spent a lot of time on the importance of listening

PAY ATTENTION TO YOUR BODY

to the voice of our bodies, of paying attention to our bodies. I believe God sometimes speaks through our bodies.

As I mentioned earlier, the body and mind are meant to work in harmony. One often affects the other. If one is addressed without paying attention to the other, lasting changes may be short-lived.

This is the subject of the next chapter.

PAY ATTENTION TO YOUR MIND AND EMOTIONS

Just as it is important to pay attention to the voice of our bodies, it is equally important to pay attention to our minds and emotions. Since our emotions are connected to our minds, then we must pay attention to how our emotions affect not only our actions, but also can affect even our bodies.

The healthier we are emotionally, the more peaceful and satisfying will be our lives. We may also find out that as we become emotionally healthy, our bodies can become healthier as well.

For a number of years as a Christian, I didn't realize how connected the body, mind and emotions are. As I began to look into that connection, I discovered that our minds hang on to experiences both good and bad.

Sometimes a bad experience early in life can have a negative impact on how we live our lives from that time on. The memories of these events can haunt us (often subconsciously) and determine how we react to people and situations.

My father was a strict disciplinarian. He would often give me and my brothers whippings for some offence. This was accompanied by angry yelling.

PAY ATTENTION

I vowed that when I became a parent, I would not do that to my children. And yet, when I had my two daughters, on a few occasions when they were beyond the toddler stage, I found myself yelling at them and administering whippings. I actually only remember spanking them one or two times during their childhood. Most of the time, I would catch myself before I fell into my father's disciplining patterns.

The Lord revealed to me that I was reacting to my children based subconsciously on the way my father reacted to me. I needed to be healed of the memories of how my father acted in order to avoid reacting the same way to my children.

We sometimes hear about children who are abused physically or sexually who grow up to become abusers themselves. Sometimes those who call themselves Christians might quote a Bible verse for beating a child. You might have heard the verse "spare the rod and spoil the child." Actually, that verse is not in the Bible. The closest to that is Proverbs 13:24, "Whoever spares the rod hates their children, but the one who loves their children is careful to discipline them." The New Living Translation reads "Those who spare the rod of discipline hate their children. Those who love their children care enough to discipline them."

PAY ATTENTION TO YOUR MIND AND EMOTIONS

I came to understand that the rod (or spankings) are only to be used judiciously and never out of anger. It should only be used as a last resort to try to discipline children. I discovered that there were other ways to discipline that might be just as effective.

If one grows up being told by parents and others that they are worthless, untalented, a failure, or any number of other such hurtful labels, those words can cause one to emotionally internalize these labels and one becomes convinced that they are true. As a result, we can tend to live up to those labels, never realizing that we are doing so.

Liam (not his real name) was a people pleaser. He lived for the love, acceptance, and approval from others. Liam was awkward socially and though he tried hard to fit in, he was not accepted by others. I came to find out that this need to please people was traced all the way back to his parents. They were never pleased with anything he did. The harder he tried, the more fault they found in him.

Once Liam was out on his own, he turned to the Lord for help. He committed his life to Christ and enrolled in seminary. Thinking he was now healed, he put on an outward appearance that he had his act together and that everything was fine.

The truth is that he never dealt with his emotional scars and memories. Though he was a Christian, Liam suffered

PAY ATTENTION

from a real depression. Liam went home one Christmas and took his own life.

Perhaps if he had paid more attention to his mind and emotions and sought help from someone who could help him identify and be healed from his past, he might still be with us.

Perhaps if those of us who were his friends paid more attention to the signs of his people pleasing attempts and depression, then we might have done something to help.

Families can often cause conflict in our minds and with our emotions. Because we are by nature and design intricately bonded with our family, we can easily be hurt in a much deeper way by family.

> A man goes on a two-month business trip to Europe and leaves his cat with his brother. Three days before his return he calls his brother. "So how's my cat doing?" the guy asks.
>
> "He's dead," his brother replies.
>
> "He's dead! What do you mean he's dead? I loved that cat. Couldn't you think of a nicer way to tell me? I'm leaving again in three days. You could have told me today she got out of the house or something. Then when I called before I left you could've told me, well, we found her but she's up on the roof and we're having trouble getting her down. Then when I call you

PAY ATTENTION TO YOUR MIND AND EMOTIONS

from the airport you could've told me the fire brigade was there and scared the cat off the roof but he died when he hit the ground."

"I'm sorry, you're right," the other brother says. "That was insensitive. I won't let it happen again."

"All right, forget about it. Anyway, how's Mom doing?"

"She's up on the roof and we're having trouble getting her down." (Taylor, 2014).

Family members, because of their insensitivity, can often say things that hurt us or cause us some type of lingering emotional pain. So, how do we handle these emotional scars?

As Christians, we become a new creation in Christ (2 Corinthians 5:17). This means that the old labels, old emotions no longer need to control us. We have the power of the Holy Spirit to overcome these negative emotions and labels.

It is not automatic that when we become Christians we can overcome these hurtful emotions, feelings and labels. Sometimes we need what is called, the healing of memories.

With the help of a mature Christian who is skilled in leading people to be healed of these past experiences and

PAY ATTENTION

hurts, one can be set free from the bondage of these hurts of the past.

There are also good books available that can help one identify and even be healed of memories of the past that continue to affect them. For example, I have found some books by John and Paula Sanford particularly helpful in the area of the healing of memories and inner healing.

PAY ATTENTION TO YOUR SPIRITUAL LIFE

As mentioned in chapter one, the essence of who we are as human beings is spiritual. We all (Christians and non-Christians) have a spirit living inside of our bodies. The spirit is that which is created in the image of God. We see a reflection of the characteristics of God in our spirits. We have the ability to love, hate, be joyful, be at peace, be patient, be kind, be good, be faithful, be gentle, and exercise self-control. These are aspects of what Paul calls the "fruit of the Spirit" (Galatians 5:22). Although our ability to manifest these characteristics is limited by sin, they are still resident in us.

Also, resident in us are what I call the "fruit of the sinful nature." Paul describes these characteristics right before he lists the fruit of the Spirit. Here is what the apostle says about our human natures.

> So, I say, walk by the Spirit, and you will not gratify the desires of the flesh [sinful nature]. For the flesh desires what is contrary to the Spirit, and the Spirit what is contrary to the flesh. They are in conflict with each other, so that you are not to do whatever you want. But if

PAY ATTENTION

> you are led by the Spirit, you are not under the law. The acts of the flesh are obvious: sexual immorality, impurity and debauchery; idolatry and witchcraft; hatred, discord, jealousy, fits of rage, selfish ambition, dissensions, factions and envy; drunkenness, orgies, and the like. I warn you, as I did before, that those who live like this will not inherit the kingdom of God.
>
> **Galatians 5:16–21**

This list of the acts of the flesh, though not comprehensive, gives the highlights of a life lived apart from the leading of the Holy Spirit. We would do well to pay attention to these sins so that we can recognize them when we are tempted to commit one and then to choose to walk in the way of obedience, the way of the Spirit.

We live in a culture and society that in various ways condones many of these acts of the flesh. These acts of the flesh are really disobedience to the commandments of God. Each of these sins fall under the category of one or more of the Ten Commandments (Exodus 20).

The Christian is called to live in a way that is obviously different from the modern cultural norms. While non-Christians and even some who would name the name of Christ believe that there is no absolute truth, no black and white, no right and wrong, Christians have the audacity to say, "There are things that are right and things that are

PAY ATTENTION TO YOUR SPIRITUAL LIFE

wrong." We say this not because we have a corner on the market of truth or that our faith makes us right, but because we have a standard of right and wrong that comes from outside of this world.

Everyone has a sense of right and wrong. Those that say that there is no absolute right or wrong will no doubt try to stop you if you try to steal their car. Why? Because they believe it is wrong to steal from them.

The Christian says, something is right or wrong, not because he says so, but because God, who is the only independent lawgiver says so. In the wrestling world there used to be a wrestler named Stone Cold Steve Austin. His catch phrase was "And that's the bottom line, because Stone Cold says so."

The bottom line of right and wrong is found in a moral lawgiver that is beyond this world. Something is right or wrong because God says so. God speaks to the behaviors and thoughts of men and women by setting out commandments that are designed to help them and those around them to live their best life by living in harmony with one another and with God.

You might say, "Well what about the commandments in the Old Testament like 'You can't eat pork or shellfish? Or you can't wear clothing made from certain materials?' There are over six hundred commandments in the Old Testament. How are we to respond to all of these commandments given to the people of Israel a few millennia ago?"

The answer to this question is the answer to many of life's questions.

> A pastor was giving the children's message during church. For this part of the service, he would gather all of the children around them before dismissing them for children's church. On this particular Sunday, he was using squirrels for an object lesson on industry and preparation. He started out by saying, "I'm going to describe something, and I want you to raise your hand when you know what it is." The children nodded eagerly. "This thing lives in trees (pause) and eats nuts (pause)…" No hands went up. "And it is gray (pause) and has a long bushy tail (pause)…" The children were looking at each other but still no hands raised. "And it jumps from branch to branch (pause) and chatters and flips its tail when it's excited (pause)…" Finally one little boy tentatively raised his hand. The pastor breathed a sign of relief and called on him. "Well," said the boy, "I know the answer must be Jesus. But it sure sounds like a squirrel!" (Stick With Jesus, 2017)

We Christians, believe the answer to many of life's questions is Jesus Christ, but when it comes to the issue of

PAY ATTENTION TO YOUR SPIRITUAL LIFE

how to respond to all of these commandments, the answer is not just Jesus, but what Jesus said in His Word, the Bible.

The apostle James said in his letter in the Bible,

> For whoever keeps the whole law but stumbles at just one point is guilty of breaking all of it. For he who said, "You shall not commit adultery," also said, "You shall not murder." If you do not commit adultery, but do commit murder, you have become a lawbreaker
> **James 2:10–11**

Here we get an insight into the law that God says we human beings are responsible for keeping. You notice it has to do with behavior. This is what the Church often calls the moral law.

There are other laws in the Old Testament that God established for the people of the old covenant (Old Testament) to follow to show their dedication and commitment to Him. But in Leviticus, the Lord reveals to the Israelites how they might be in right relationship to Him as His covenant people. How could they approach this awesome God the right way? How could they worship Him and walk in relationship with Him? The book of Leviticus was the answer to those questions, albeit within the context of the Mosaic covenant established at Sinai between God and Israel.

Some of these commandments were a foreshadowing of something that was ultimately fulfilled by Jesus Christ.

PAY ATTENTION

For example, the priests were commanded by God to offer animal sacrifices on the altar of the temple to cover over the sins of the people. Jesus Christ's sacrifice of His life on the cross did away with the need for animal sacrifices on an altar, because He was sacrificed by His Father in heaven (foreshadowed by Abraham and Isaac) on the altar of the cross. John describes Jesus as "the Lamb of God who takes away the sin of the world" (John 1:29).

There are four main types of laws in the Old Testament, and indeed, the New as well. There are ceremonial laws. The ceremonial laws are rules that apply mainly to worship. They are found in Leviticus and the other books of Moses. These laws, for example, detail how the various sacrifices were to be offered, how ceremonies were to be performed, how the temple and tabernacle were to be constructed, and how to worship God. It also gave instructions concerning who was authorized to do what in the tabernacle or temple and what their qualifications were and how they were organized.

The next type of law found in the Old Testament is what we might call the civil law. The Jews believed in a theocracy: a government under God. God gave various civil laws (or instructed His leaders to so do) for the governance of the people of Israel. The civil law deals mainly with relationships between individuals, the settling of dis-

PAY ATTENTION TO YOUR SPIRITUAL LIFE

putes, and the description of proper behavior. Things like punishments for Sabbath breaking, unpaid debt, divorce, unjust practices, not dealing justly with the poor, using unjust scales in commerce, and the like. These laws were ultimately fulfilled in Jesus Christ, and He often spoke to issues like these. The civil laws often prescribed the punishments for breaking the moral laws.

The third type of law is what we might call the dietary law. In the Old Testament, God established that certain foods were forbidden to be eaten. Though it would take them awhile to get there, because of their disobedience, the Israelites were on their way to the land of Canaan, in order to possess the land from the pagan Canaanites. And the Lord was calling them to be distinct in their behavior, to separate themselves from the pagan rituals and practices of the surrounding nations, and in so doing, to reflect God's holiness.

One of the ways they could demonstrate that separation was in what they ate. Their diet would be noticeably different from the pagan nations around them; and as such it would serve as a daily reminder, at every meal, that they were God's holy people.

So, that meant no bacon cheeseburgers, no shrimp alfredo, no clam chowder, and no crab cakes, but instead a constant reminder for them that they had been separated

PAY ATTENTION

unto God, and a continual testimony to the nations around them that because the Israelites were God's people, they were different, even when it came to what they ate.

Jesus also came to fulfill this law. Statements made by Jesus show that these laws and the keeping of them did not make one more holy. He said things like this in passages like Matthew 15:11, "What goes into someone's mouth does not defile them, but what comes out of their mouth, that is what defiles them."

Jesus commands Peter in Acts 10:15–19 to eat all of the animals considered unclean by the Jews and the dietary laws. Following the teachings of Jesus, Paul says,

> Therefore do not let anyone judge you by what you eat or drink, or with regard to a religious festival, a New Moon celebration or a Sabbath day. These are a shadow of the things that were to come; the reality, however, is found in Christ.
> **Colossians 2:16–17**

If Jesus fulfilled and did away with these dietary restrictions, how are we to view them today? Many people see God's wisdom in restricting the eating of these forbidden foods. As modern science looks at the benefits of different foods, many of the "forbidden foods" turn out to be not so good for us. Some would want to mandate that Christians abstain from these foods, but God has left the

PAY ATTENTION TO YOUR SPIRITUAL LIFE

choice to eat or abstain up to the Christian.

In light of the theme of this book, we would do well to pay attention to what we eat and drink. As Paul says in 1 Corinthians 10:31 "So whether you eat or drink or whatever you do, do it all for the glory of God."

The fourth type of law found in the Old Testament (and indeed in the New Testament) is what we might call the moral law. Moral laws in the Old Testament were not given only to the theocracy of Israel but these were laws based on God's character and His design for His creation in this world. Many of these laws were known orally for thousands of years before Moses ever wrote them into the laws of the Mosaic covenant.

Moral laws in the Old Testament are presented in one of two ways. They are either a positive or negative command that stands alone like "do this" or "don't do that" or they are sometimes found inside civil laws like "if you do this then the punishment or restitution for doing that is this."

Examples of this law would include but are not limited to commands regarding murder, children honoring and obeying their parents, adultery, covetousness and theft.

The Church has always taught that these moral laws were not just for the people of Israel, but were laws established by God for all generations. When these laws were given, many Jews believed that they would not be accepted by God if they didn't obey these commandments.

Paul says in Galatians 3:24: "So the law was our guardian until Christ came that we might be justified by faith." The New Living Translation puts it this way, "The law was our guardian until Christ came; it protected us until we could be made right with God through faith."

So, the Christian understanding of the moral law is that it was given by God to show people His character and what standard He would be using to judge them. It was also given to show people the impossibility of living a perfectly moral life in their own strength and power. Jesus came along to fulfill the law and the prophets (Matthew 5:17).

Jesus fulfilled the moral law not only by affirming it and seeking to adhere to it, but He in fact perfectly kept the moral law. Thus, Jesus was without sin (Hebrews 4:15).

While it is important for the Christian to pay attention to the moral law, the attempts to keep the law will not result in one's salvation. Salvation can only happen as one puts his faith in the One who lived the perfect life we could not live, and trust that His sacrifice on the cross paid the price for his sins.

The apostle Paul puts it this way,

> For it is by grace you have been saved, through

PAY ATTENTION TO YOUR SPIRITUAL LIFE

> faith— and this not from yourselves, it is the gift of God— not by works, so that no one can boast. For we are God's handiwork, created in Christ Jesus to do good works, which God prepared in advance for us to do.
> **Ephesians 2:8–10**

So, salvation comes through our faith in the finished work of Christ on the cross and His resurrection.

According to Paul, the good works we do are a result of our salvation as we work out that salvation by right behavior and right actions. The word for God's handiwork in the Greek is *poema* from which we get the word poem. God is writing His poem through our lives as we do and say the things that He wants is to do and say. While we are on this earth we will never fully be able to do the good works or good behavior because of the spiritual battle we have with our sinful natures. We also are battling what the Bible calls the unbiblical philosophies of this world and the lies of the devil (see Ephesians 6:11–12; 1 John 2:15,17; James 3:13–15).

If we can't consistently keep the moral law in our own strength and power, what hope do we have? What is the use in trying to obey? Throughout the Bible, God calls His people to obey His commandments. Jesus said, "If you love me, keep my [moral] commandments" (John 14:15).

PAY ATTENTION

However, trying to obey in our own strength and power is not only futile, it is frustrating. God knew all along that we could not fully obey His commandments. He certainly knew we could not save ourselves or be good enough for salvation on our own.

He had a plan. God speaks through the prophet Ezekiel,

> For I will take you out of the nations; I will gather you from all the countries and bring you back into your own land. I will sprinkle clean water on you, and you will be clean; I will cleanse you from all your impurities and from all your idols. I will give you a new heart and put a new spirit in you; I will remove from you your heart of stone and give you a heart of flesh. And I will put my Spirit in you and move you to follow my decrees and be careful to keep my laws.
> **Ezekiel 36:24–27**

God's plan was to give His children a way to obey His commandments, not to earn their salvation, but to live a righteous life. A person becomes a child of God when they believe in and receive Jesus as their savior (John 1:14). As mentioned earlier, when they receive Jesus, the Holy Spirit is sent to live inside of the believer. He, the Holy Spirit, begins the process of transforming the human spirit. Our spirits are initially made acceptable to God (justification)

PAY ATTENTION TO YOUR SPIRITUAL LIFE

and then the Spirit begins to develop the characteristics of God's moral nature within us (sanctification).

This is what God means when He says through Ezekiel,

> I will cleanse you from all your impurities and from all your idols. I will give you a new heart and put a new spirit in you; I will remove from you your heart of stone and give you a heart of flesh.
> **Ezekiel 36:25–26**

That is salvation. Jesus refers to this as being "born again."

The next step God takes in the life of the believer is what is called the sanctification process. God does this by moving us, by His Spirit, to follow His decrees and (pay attention) be careful to keep His laws. As the Spirit gives us the power to obey God's commandments, He also begins to develop within us the characteristics that will serve to help us continue to follow and obey His commandments. These characteristics are called the fruit of the Spirit. Saint Paul described this spiritual fruit when he wrote:

> But the fruit of the Spirit is love, joy, peace, forbearance, kindness, goodness, faithfulness, gentleness and self-control. Against such things there is no law. Those who belong to Christ Je-

PAY ATTENTION

sus have crucified the flesh with its passions and desires. Since we live by the Spirit, let us keep in step with the Spirit. Let us not become conceited, provoking and envying each other.
Galatians 5:22

This is not an exhaustive list of godly characteristics but is meant to show that we have two natures. We have a sinful nature. That part of our being that tends to rebel, disobey, and break the commandments of God. We also have a righteous nature. That part of our being that tends to want to do the right thing and to follow the commandments of God.

Because we have part of the spiritual nature of God, we all (Christians and non-Christians) can at times act, speak, and do things that reflect the nature of God. This, however, is not our natural proclivity. Our human natures are corrupted by sin to the point that we tend to act selfishly if left to our own devices.

Depending on whether we have been born again of the Spirit (John 3:6) and how much we are submitted to the Spirit's leading, we have the chance to better reflect those good characteristics of God. This is called by Saint Paul, "walking in the Spirit" (Romans 8).

So, when I speak of the spiritual life in Christian terms, I am speaking about how we act, speak and behave. This spiritual life affects our relationships with ourselves, others and with God.

PAY ATTENTION TO YOUR SPIRITUAL LIFE

One thing the Christian soon learns is that there is a war going on inside of them. It is easily described as a battle between good and evil. It is more than that, it is a battle between the good Spirit of God within us and the sinful human spirit that seeks to not submit to God, His commandments and His will.

God has given us what theologians call free will. That is, we have the freedom to obey or disobey God. We are not puppets under the direction of a cosmic Geppetto.

As a result, if we are not a Christian, we can occasionally without thinking about it act, speak, and behave in a way that is consistent with commandments and will of God. But normally, the non-Christian reverts back to the direction of the sinful nature.

For the Christian, the Holy Spirit is living inside of them and is seeking to move the believer in the direction of obedience to God's will and commandments. He (the Spirit) will not override or make one do something but will try to inspire the believer to obedience, often by reminding him of the written Word of God or in the voice of the Spirit through the conscience.

As one becomes more proficient at walking in the Spirit, this process becomes more natural and effortless. It is not a matter so much of will power, but rather a matter of the Spirit's power (Zechariah 4:6).

PAY ATTENTION

By God putting His Spirit in us, we have a new power to overcome the sinful human spirit within us. That spirit (or heart as it is called in the Ezekiel passage above) becomes more malleable (a heart of flesh) under the Spirit's direction. Along with that, God says He will, by His Spirit, move us follow His will and be better able to keep His commandments.

Of course, this is where the battle between what the Bible calls the *flesh* and the *spirit* has the ability to turn in a more righteous direction. God promises to, by His Spirit, move (inspire us) to be more aware and open to acting, speaking, and behaving according to His will and commandments.

While the Christian has the Holy Spirit living inside of them, they may not actually be utilizing the Spirit's power to help them to follow God's decrees and be careful to keep His laws.

Even the great apostle Paul struggled with this in his life. Listen to how he describes this inner struggle:

> We know that the law is spiritual; but I am unspiritual, sold as a slave to sin. I do not understand what I do. For what I want to do I do not do, but what I hate I do. And if I do what I do not want to do, I agree that the law is good. As it is, it is no longer I myself who do it, but it

PAY ATTENTION TO YOUR SPIRITUAL LIFE

is sin living in me. For I know that good itself does not dwell in me, that is, in my sinful nature. For I have the desire to do what is good, but I cannot carry it out. For I do not do the good I want to do, but the evil I do not want to do—this I keep on doing Now if I do what I do not want to do, it is no longer I who do it, but it is sin living in me that does it. So, I find this law at work: Although I want to do good, evil is right there with me. For in my inner being I delight in God's law; but I see another law at work in me, waging war against the law of my mind and making me a prisoner of the law of sin at work within me. What a wretched man I am! Who will rescue me from this body that is subject to death?

Romans 7:14–24

Paul, who had seen Jesus on the road to Damascus, who had been filled with the Holy Spirit, still faced an inner struggle between his renewed spiritual nature and his sinful nature. The great apostle not only knew that he had to pay attention to the direction of the Spirit and that he had to acknowledge he could not do that in his own power.

What did he do? He focused his attention on the only one who could rescue him from the struggles that he faced. He concludes by saying in answer to his question, who will rescue me from this body that is subject to death? "Thanks be to God, who delivers me through Jesus Christ our Lord!" (Romans 7:25).

PAY ATTENTION

Paul realized that he needed to pay attention to the Lord Jesus working through the Holy Spirit. But that knowledge was not enough. He needed the knowledge infused with power.

The Christian may well know that they need Jesus and the Holy Spirit to have any hope of living a godly, righteous life, but just knowing that doesn't bring it to reality.

I know the computer on which I am working right now has a lot of power to do word processing, internet surfing, file storage, and many other things, but if I don't connect it to the source of power, it won't do anything for me.

The reason why many Christians have such a hard time living the Christian life, is because they have not yet unleashed the power of the Spirit within them to allow them to be able to do what the Spirit desires them to do.

When I was growing up we had a gas stove. The stove had a pilot light that was always burning. The burner coils on the stove remained cool and unable to heat up anything until the control knob on the stove was turned on. When that happened, there was an initial hiss followed by a woosh as the gas sent the flame from the pilot light to the burner coils. It was then that the stove actually functioned as it was designed. It had the power to cook something.

This analogy describes, in my opinion and experience, the missing ingredient in the life of the average Christian.

PAY ATTENTION TO YOUR SPIRITUAL LIFE

This missing ingredient is referred to in the Bible in different ways. It is best described by Jesus as "the promise of the Father."

Listen to how the book of Acts quotes Jesus' words:

> On one occasion, while he was eating with them, he gave them this command: "Do not leave Jerusalem, but wait for the gift my Father promised, which you have heard me speak about. For John baptized with water, but in a few days you will be baptized with the Holy Spirit."
>
> **Acts 1:4–5**

In order for us to understand what Jesus is talking about we have to do some backtracking. When Jesus was baptized in the Jordan River by John the Baptist, it was not because Jesus needed baptism for repentance or for the cleansing of sin. Jesus was already completely sin free and already had the Holy Spirit living in him (after all He was conceived by the Holy Spirit in the womb of the Virgin Mary).

Jesus did many things to show His followers what they needed to do. Jesus' baptism was a vivid picture of what would one day become the experience of the apostles and disciples of Jesus.

PAY ATTENTION

Jesus had not yet begun the ministry to which He was called to accomplish by His Father. Even though Jesus had been growing in "wisdom and stature, and in favor with God and man" (Luke 2:52), he had not yet been empowered to take on the plan of God to become the Savior of the world.

Jesus demonstrated for His followers that just as He needed to be empowered for His ministry, so too, would they need to be empowered.

When Jesus was baptized, the Holy Spirit descended upon Him in the form of a dove. We can sometimes be confused by this image.

> A preacher came up with a unique way of emphasizing the coming of the Holy Spirit upon the Church. He placed the janitor in the balcony with a dove. The janitor was instructed to release the dove over the congregation at just the right moment in the worship service. The preacher said, "Now when you hear me say that the Holy Spirit came down out of heaven like a dove, I want you to release the dove." The following Sunday everything was ready, and the preacher reached the point in the sermon he had carefully planned. In his sermon he said, "And the Spirit of God came down like a dove." Nothing happened. Raising his hand and calling out somewhat louder, the preacher declared, "And the Spirit came down like a dove."

PAY ATTENTION TO YOUR SPIRITUAL LIFE

> Still nothing happened. Finally, the preacher raised both hands and strained his voice to say once more, "And the Spirit came down like a dove." Just then the janitor called out from the balcony, "Pastor, the cat ate the [Holy Spirit], do you want me to throw down the cat?" (Minnix, n.d.)

The Holy Spirit is not a dove (or a cat), but the Spirit came in a physical manifestation so that John the Baptist and those witnessing Jesus' baptism would recognize that something special was happening to the Savior.

Just as the dove brought back a sign of new life on the earth that had been flooded during the time of Noah, now the Holy Spirit was descending on Jesus as a sign of the new life He would bring.

In the Old Testament and in the beginning of the New Testament, the Holy Spirit was not living inside of believers but was living with them.

Jesus said this,

> If you love me, keep my commands. And I will ask the Father, and he will give you another advocate to help you and be with you forever— the Spirit of truth. The world cannot accept him, because it neither sees him nor knows him. But you know him, for he lives with you and will be in you.
>
> **John 14:15–17**

PAY ATTENTION

Throughout the Old Testament all the way through the day of Pentecost, the Spirit "came upon" particular people for particular tasks at particular times. This coming upon was a foreshadowing of the Holy Spirit coming upon Jesus and later on the apostles and disciples of Jesus.

It's important to observe that in the Old Testament the Spirit was not living in people the way He would eventually do in the New Testament. He doesn't indwell everyone. Rather the Spirit "comes upon" or "fills" only specific people for a special service. For example:

Bezalel is "filled" with the Spirit of God to develop and execute artistic designs for the tabernacle (Exodus 31:2; 35:31). *The 70 Elders* receive some of the Spirit of God that is on Moses (Numbers 11:17, 25). *Gideon* is able to deliver Israel because "the Spirit of the Lord came on Gideon" (Judges 6:34), as well as upon other judges (Judges 3:10; 11:29). *Samson* performs feats of strength when the Spirit of the Lord comes upon him (Judges 13:25; 14:6, 19; 15:14).

Prophets prophesy when the Spirit of God comes upon them (2 Chronicles 15:1; 20:14; 24:20; Joel 2:28–29; Luke 2:25).

The filling of a person with the Holy Spirit is the gift about which Jesus was speaking in Acts 1. It is a continuation of how the Holy Spirit worked in the lives of cer-

PAY ATTENTION TO YOUR SPIRITUAL LIFE

tain people in the Old Testament. Just as the Holy Spirit had come upon certain people, at certain times, for certain tasks, Jesus was saying that His followers were to receive this power as well.

Jesus also alluded to this gift in Luke 24:49: "I am going to send you what my Father has promised; but stay in the city until you have been clothed with power from on Jesus said this to apostles and disciples forty days after His resurrection and right before He ascended into heaven to return to the place from which He originally came when He laid aside all of the rights and privileges of being God and humbled Himself to become a human being (Philippians 2). Before He ascended He was telling His followers that they were still lacking something.

What could they be lacking? They already had received the promise of John 14. The Holy Spirit was already living inside of them. In John's Gospel, Jesus made one of His post-resurrection appearances to His apostles.

> On the evening of that first day of the week, when the disciples were together, with the doors locked for fear of the Jewish leaders, Jesus came and stood among them and said, "Peace be with you!" After he said this, he showed them his hands and side. The disciples were overjoyed when they saw the Lord. Again, Jesus said, "Peace be with you! As the Father has

sent me, I am sending you." And with that he breathed on them and said, "Receive the Holy Spirit."

John 20:19–22

This is reminiscent of the creation of man when Moses writes in the book of Genesis, "Then the LORD God formed man from the dust of the ground and breathed the breath of life into his nostrils, and the man became a living being," (Genesis 2:7). The Hebrew word used here for breath is the word which can also be translated spirit. So, God breathed into Adam a human spirit and he became a living being.

Now, Jesus was breathing (imparting) the Holy Spirit into His followers. They "received" the Holy Spirit. They became "born again" (See the story of Nicodemus in John 3) and were now children of God and fully Christians. They had now become a new creation in Christ. Their sins were forgiven, they have a new life in Christ and eternity in their hearts as they await their departure from this earth at their death or at the return of Jesus to begin eternal life in His presence and kingdom.

As we look at the above passages, we begin to see that even though the apostles and disciples had the Holy Spirit living within them, mingling with their human spirits and beginning the process of redeeming those sinful human spirits, they were still lacking something. They were "pilot light" Christians who needed the gas turned on.

PAY ATTENTION TO YOUR SPIRITUAL LIFE

Again, in Luke 24, Jesus tells His followers that in order to receive what they were lacking, they needed to wait in Jerusalem "until you have been clothed with power from on high." This power from on high is the same as the promise of the Father to which Jesus referred in Acts 1.

This promise of the Father is also called the "baptism in or with the Holy Spirit." This baptism is different from water baptism. It is assumed that the apostles and disciples of Jesus were already baptized in water via "John's baptism." One reason I say they were already baptized is that John 4:2 says that Jesus disciples were baptizing many. One can assume that the "disciples" doing the baptisms here include or are exclusively the apostles. It seems very unlikely that Jesus would have had His apostles baptize those who believed in Him if they had not themselves been baptized. I would guess that most scholars would agree that the apostles were baptized by either John or Jesus.

So, when Jesus was talking about a baptism with the Spirit, He was describing an experience He Himself had at His water baptism (remember, He already had the Holy Spirit living in Him when He was baptized). His followers (who already had the Holy Spirit living in them) were to wait for the missing ingredient that they would need to be better able to live the Christian life, perform their ministries and be effective witnesses for Jesus.

PAY ATTENTION

As Jesus ascended into heaven, those who had received His command to wait in Jerusalem until they had been clothed with power from on high, went to an upper room in Jerusalem to wait for what Jesus promised. They waited ten more days before anything happened. They prayed in expectation of something happening to them.

That something occurred during the Jewish festival of Pentecost. It was a time when Jews (who were able) were required to come from all over the world to Jerusalem to celebrate this annual event. The term Pentecost comes from the Greek Πεντηκοστή (*Pentēkostē*) meaning "fiftieth". It refers to the festival celebrated on the fiftieth day after Passover, also known as the "Feast of Weeks" and the "Feast of Fifty days" in rabbinic tradition.

As the apostles and disciples were awaiting this promise of the Father, this baptism with the Holy Spirit, they had no idea what was about to happen.

Here is how Luke describes what happened.

> When the day of Pentecost came, they were all together in one place. Suddenly a sound like the blowing of a violent wind came from heaven and filled the whole house where they were sitting. They saw what seemed to be tongues of fire that separated and came to rest on each of them. All of them were filled with the Holy Spirit and began to speak in other tongues as the Spirit enabled them.
>
> **Acts 2:1–3**

PAY ATTENTION TO YOUR SPIRITUAL LIFE

Just as the Holy Spirit had come upon Jesus at His baptism, that same Spirit came upon Jesus' apostles and disciples not in the form of a dove, but as a mighty rushing wind and tongues of fire. They were *all* filled with the Holy Spirit.

They began to speak in tongues. In this case, the tongues were known languages as evidenced by the fact that those who heard them speaking heard their own languages being spoken. These Jews and God-fearing Gentiles who heard them speak were probably outside of the room in which the disciples were gathered and realized that these who were speaking, "were Galileans." The crowd probably thought that these were uneducated people who could not have learned other languages. These upon whom the Spirit had fallen were proclaiming the wonders of God in languages they had never learned.

The people who were hearing them speaking in tongues must have thought these disciples of Jesus were drunk. Peter had to assure the crowd that these disciples were not drunk, after all it was only 9 o'clock in the morning (Acts 2:15).

Those who were speaking in these languages reflect one aspect of the spiritual gift of speaking in tongues. The other aspect of speaking in tongues is seen in St. Paul's first letter to the Corinthians. Paul describes the spiritual gift of speaking in tongues in a different way. He says that when a

PAY ATTENTION

Christian is speaking in tongues, they are "not speaking to people but to God. Indeed, no one understands them; they utter mysteries by the Spirit" (1 Corinthians 14:2).

If "no one understands them" then these tongues must be a language that is other than human. Paul says this of the different types of tongues (known and unknown) when he says, "If I speak in the tongues of men or of angels, but do not have love, I am only a resounding gong or a clanging cymbal" (1 Corinthians 13:1).

The tongues that were spoken on the day of Pentecost were known languages. Evidently, when some people were filled with the Holy Spirit in New Testament times they were able to speak in languages that they had not learned (tongues of men or of angels).

If these languages were being spoken by Jesus' followers, they were either done in public or in private. If they were spoken in private, then it seems Paul was talking about a person's personal prayer. He says this in 1 Corinthians 14:4: "Anyone who speaks in a tongue edifies themselves [builds up their spiritual life], but the one who prophesies edifies the church. I would like every one of you to speak in tongues." So, Paul wants all believers to speak in tongues.

He goes on to give instructions related to the public use of this gift of speaking in tongues. "…but I would rather

PAY ATTENTION TO YOUR SPIRITUAL LIFE

have you prophesy. The one who prophesies is greater than the one who speaks in tongues, unless someone interprets, so that the church may be edified."

In the church worship service, Paul encourages speaking in tongues only if there is someone who can interpret the tongues (the gift of the interpretation of tongues). The reason for this is that if there is an unbeliever in the congregation, that unbeliever will think the speaker is just babbling. Not only that, but the believers need to hear the interpretation so that their faith would be built up (edified).

Paul continues in verse 14: "For if I pray in a tongue, my spirit prays, but my mind is unfruitful." The apostle is describing what speaking in tongues is. When one speaks in a tongue (or unknown language) it is really the Holy Spirit speaking to the Father through the speaker. The speaker is speaking the words, but they remain unknown to the speaker unless he or someone else has the gift of the interpretation of tongues and interprets what is being spoken.

What should one do? Paul says, "So, what shall I do? I will pray with my spirit, but I will also pray with my understanding; I will sing with my spirit, but I will also sing with my understanding" (1 Corinthians 14:15). The one filled with the Holy Spirit is to pray in their normal language, but also pray "in the Spirit." They are to use all means of prayer to fully communicate with God.

Much of praying in the Spirit is really simply praising and thanking God.

> Otherwise when you are praising God in the Spirit, how can someone else, who is now put in the position of an inquirer, say 'Amen' to your thanksgiving, since they do not know what you are saying? You are giving thanks well enough, but no one else is edified.
> **1 Corinthians 14:16–17**

When you are praying in the Spirit (speaking in tongues) in private, much of what you are doing is praising and thanking God in a way beyond the limitations of your human language. It could very well be that praying in tongues gives the Holy Spirit the chance to pray for something or someone's needs that you might not even be aware of. When you are praying in the Spirit in public, you may be praising and thanking God well enough, but others won't understand what you are praying unless there is a public interpretation.

This is not to say the one filled with the Holy Spirit could not speak in a known language (like on the Day of Pentecost). There are many anecdotal stories of Christians speaking in a known language, and an unbeliever recognizes that language as their own native language. John

PAY ATTENTION TO YOUR SPIRITUAL LIFE

Sherrill's book contains many such stories. Paul is not giving some theological teaching, but rather a practical teaching. It is one with which he is intimately familiar. "I thank God that I speak in tongues more than all of you. But in the church I would rather speak five intelligible words to instruct others than ten thousand words in a tongue" (1 Corinthians 14:18–19).

If Paul speaks in tongues more than all to whom he is writing, and yet, his preferred method of speaking is in understandable language, then where is he speaking in tongues? The inference is that he speaks in tongues mainly in private, during his personal prayer times.

So important is speaking in tongues in the life of the believer that he says,

> What then shall we say, brothers and sisters? When you come together, each of you has a hymn, or a word of instruction, a revelation, a tongue or an interpretation. Everything must be done so that the church may be built up. If anyone speaks in a tongue, two—or at the most three—should speak, one at a time, and someone must interpret. If there is no interpreter, the speaker should keep quiet in the church and speak to himself and to God.
> **1 Corinthians 14:26–28**

PAY ATTENTION

Did you catch that? If a believer feels they should speak in tongues in church and there is no interpretation or interpreter there, then that person should keep quiet in the church and "speak to himself and to God." Speaking in tongues is not a badge of spiritual maturity or superiority, but rather another way for one to pray to build himself up and to pray to God.

I would also add that one should not speak in tongues in church if the majority of the believers there have never been baptized or fill with the Holy Spirit. Such speaking would only cause division and confusion.

Why have I spent so much time on this particular gift of the Spirit? Mainly because many in the church have a misunderstanding about this gift and even a fear of the gift. Until one experiences this gift, it remains a mystery, and he does not really see the need of receiving or using the gift of speaking in tongues.

There is also a teaching out there that says you are not baptized or filled with the Holy Spirit unless you speak in tongues. While it is true that this gift is often the first manifestation or evidence of one being filled with the Holy Spirit, it is not the only evidence. One may be filled with the Holy Spirit and not speak in tongues. That may be a relief to many reading these words.

However, if this gift seems in Scripture to be associat-

PAY ATTENTION TO YOUR SPIRITUAL LIFE

ed with being filled with the Spirit, then why wouldn't one want to receive this gift?

Perhaps one reason is that we have been conditioned against speaking in tongues or praying in the Spirit by a mischaracterization of this gift in television and movies. In the movie Cape Fear starring Robert DeNiro, he plays a crazy person who "speaks in tongues" and threatens a lawyer and his family.

Sometimes a Christian church or minister will be portrayed in the media in a negative light by showing the congregation speaking in tongues and appearing a bit mindless. These people portray being given over to ecstasy, but not in a good way.

If this gift of speaking in tongues is legitimate and is a part of the spiritual armor of the Christian, then why would one not want to receive what God wants to give them? If this is a gift from God, then would God give us something that is not good for us?

Jesus said on one occasion "If you, then, though you are evil, know how to give *good gifts* to your children, how much more will your Father in heaven give *good gifts* to those who ask him!" (Matthew 7:11 emphasis added).

Jesus may have put it a different way on another occasion when He said, "If you, then, though you are evil, know how to give good gifts to your children, how much more will your Father in heaven give the Holy Spirit to those who ask him!" (Luke 11:13).

The baptism with the Holy Spirit is available to every believer. The gifts of the Spirit are also available to every believer who is filled with the Holy Spirit. Paul says this,

> There are different gifts, but the same Spirit distributes them. There are different kinds of service [ministries], but the same Lord. There are different kinds of working, but in all of them and in everyone it the same God at work. Now to each one the manifestation of the Spirit is given for the common good. To one there is through the Spirit the message of wisdom, to another the message of knowledge by means of the same Spirit, to another faith by the same Spirit, to another gifts of healing by that one Spirit, to another miraculous powers, to another prophecy, to another distinguishing between spirits, to another speaking in different kinds tongues, and to still another the interpretation of tongues. All these are the work of one and the same Spirit, and he distributes them to each one as he determines.
> **1 Corinthians 12:4–11**

In fact, Paul says that we are to be filled with the Holy Spirit, "Do not get *drunk* on *wine*, which leads to debauchery. Instead, be filled with the Spirit, speaking to one another with psalms, hymns, and songs from the Spir-

PAY ATTENTION TO YOUR SPIRITUAL LIFE

it" (Ephesians 5:18–19). The Greek word he uses is in the continuous sense. In other words, we are to be continually filled with the Holy Spirit. This is not just a one-time experience. It seems reasonable that this singing songs from the Spirit would be singing in tongues.

Since as St. Paul says in 2 Corinthians, we have the spiritual treasure of the presence of Christ and His Spirit living in our jars of clay, then it seems that these jars can leak, meaning we need to be constantly filled (or refilled) with the Holy Spirit.

Often, the first time a person is filled with the Holy Spirit, that person experiences something that lets them know they have been filled. Some may be filled with an unusual joy, or an overwhelming peace. Some may speak in tongues, some may receive an immediate manifestation of a gift of the Spirit. Just as the apostles and disciples knew they were filled with the Holy Spirit on the day of Pentecost, so too, I believe will a person know when they are first filled with the Spirit.

However, subsequent fillings with the Holy Spirit may come without any outward manifestations or feelings.

How is one filled with the Holy Spirit? The first step is to believe in Jesus Christ as your savior and to invite Him into your heart. "If you declare with your mouth, 'Jesus is Lord,' and believe in your heart that God raised Him from the dead, you will be saved… for everyone who calls on the name of the Lord will be saved" (Romans 10:9, 13). When you invite Jesus into your heart you are following what is reflected in Revelation 3:20 "Here I am! I stand at the door and knock. If anyone hears my voice and opens the door, I will come in and eat with that person and they with me."

Holman Hunt, the Raphaelite painter, is known for one of his famous paintings depicted Jesus standing at a door overgrown with vines. He is holding a lantern and appears to be knocking at the door. The unusual thing about this scene is that there is no door knob or handle on the outside of the door. The implication is that Jesus will not force His way into the house but will come in by invitation only.

When we open the door of our hearts and invite Jesus to come in to be our Savior and Lord (ruler), He will come in and eat with us (have fellowship and a relationship with us).

He comes to live inside of us, in the essence of our being (our spirits), by His Holy Spirit. We become children of God at this point.

> Yet to all who did receive him, to those who believed in his name, he gave the right to become children of God—children born not of natural descent, nor of human decision or a husband's will, but born of God.
> **John 1:12**

PAY ATTENTION TO YOUR SPIRITUAL LIFE

When you invite Christ into your life, He will send the Holy Spirit to live inside of you and the Spirit Himself will testify with your spirit that you are God's child (Romans 8:16). According to the Bible, even though all human beings are made in the image of God, not all are children of God. Only those who have the Holy Spirit mingling with their human spirits are truly children of God.

As we noted earlier, when we invite Jesus to come into our lives, our sinful human spirits are reborn, they are "born again." We become a new creation in Christ and we have a new relationship with God who views us through the sacrifice of Christ on the cross. God sees us justified (just as if we had not sinned) before Him. We have eternal life with Christ, a home in heaven, and a promise to receive a new resurrection body when Christ returns at His second coming.

Once we have become Christians and are born again, we are still missing something. We are missing the power of the Spirit to help us to live a better Christian life, more power to recognize and resist sin, and more power to effectively minister and witness for Christ.

We need to be baptized with or in the Holy Spirit. Let's look at some examples of people being filled with the Holy I've mentioned previously how the disciples and apostles were filled with the Holy Spirit on the day of Pentecost.

PAY ATTENTION

That wasn't the only occasion in the New Testament where the Holy Spirit came upon people.

When Peter and John were released from Jewish custody They

> ...went back to their own people and reported all that the chief priests and the elders had said to them. When they heard this, they raised their voices together in prayer to God. 'Sovereign Lord,' they said, 'you made the heavens and the earth and the sea, and everything in them. You spoke by the Holy Spirit through the mouth of your servant, our father David: Why do the nations rage, and the peoples plot in vain? The kings of the earth rise up and the rulers band together against the Lord and against his anointed one. Indeed, Herod and Pontius Pilate met together with the Gentiles and the people of Israel in this city to conspire against your holy servant Jesus, whom you anointed. They did what your power and will had decided beforehand should happen. Now, Lord, consider their threats and enable your servants to speak your word with great boldness. Stretch out your hand to heal and perform signs and wonders through the name of your holy servant Jesus.' After they prayed, the place where they were meeting was shaken. And they were all filled with the Holy Spirit and spoke the word of God boldly.
> **Acts 4:23–31**

PAY ATTENTION TO YOUR SPIRITUAL LIFE

In this instance, the Holy Spirit came upon the believers after they prayed. This helps us to know that the same apostles and disciples who were filled with the Holy Spirit on the day of Pentecost were now filled again with the Spirit. There is no indication that they spoke in tongues on this occasion, but they did speak the word of God boldly.

In Acts 8, we read the story of Simon the Sorcerer. He had many followers who did so because he was a good magician. A Christian named Philip came and preached the good news to the people of Samaria (many of whom were followers of Simon). Philip baptized many into the Christian faith. Even Simon was baptized and was astonished by the miracles and signs of God's kingdom performed by Philip.

When the apostles in Jerusalem heard that the word of God was accepted by many in Samaria, they sent Peter and John to them. When these apostles arrived, they prayed for these new believers that they would receive the Holy Spirit, because the Holy Spirit had not yet *come upon* any of them, they had simply been baptized in the name of the Lord Jesus.

As an aside, if these new believers had received Jesus and were baptized as Christians then the Holy Spirit would already be living inside of them, yet they still lacked something.

PAY ATTENTION

"Then Peter and John placed their hands on them, and they received the Holy Spirit" (Acts 8:17). We know that something happened to these new believers when Peter and John laid their hands on them because Simon saw something happening to them.

Perhaps these new believers were speaking in tongues, maybe they were filled with joy, maybe they were exhibiting some other outward sign that something had happened to them. We know this because Simon the Sorcerer wanted to acquire the power to make people do what these believing Samaritans were doing.

> When Simon saw that the Spirit was given at the laying on of the apostles' hands, he offered them money and said, "Give me also this ability so that everyone on whom I lay my hands may receive the Holy Spirit."
> **Acts 8:18–19**

The next account of the baptism with or in the Holy Spirit is seen in Acts 9. Before he was known as Saint Paul, the apostle was known as Saul of Tarsus. He was a Jewish Pharisee who took his religion very seriously. So much so that he appealed to the Jewish leaders to send him on a mission find and arrest Christians (whom he believed were threatening their Jewish faith and practice). Saul was present as the first recorded martyr of the church, Stephen, was

PAY ATTENTION TO YOUR SPIRITUAL LIFE

sentenced to death. Saul gave his approval to Stephen's stoning even having Stephen's clothes laid at Saul's feet.

As Saul was on the road to Damascus to seek out and arrest more Christians,

> ...suddenly a light from heaven flashed around him. He fell to the ground and heard a voice say to him, "Saul, Saul, why do you persecute me?" "Who are you, Lord?" Saul asked. "I am Jesus, whom you are persecuting," he replied. "Now get up and go into the city, and you will be told what you must do.
> **Acts 9:1–6**

Paul then saw Jesus (1 Corinthians 9:1). Saul was blinded by this experience and was led into town.

A follower of Jesus named Ananias was instructed by God to go find Saul and lay hands on him to receive his sight again and for something else to happen. When Ananias arrived at the place where Saul was staying, he went into him and

> Placing his hands on Saul, he said, "Brother Saul, the Lord—Jesus, who appeared to you on the road as you were coming here—has sent me so that you may see again and be filled with the Holy Spirit"
> **Acts 9:17**

PAY ATTENTION

Saul's eyes were opened, and he could see again, and he was baptized in water. Seeing the transformation in Saul, we can assume that he was also filled with the Holy Spirit.

The next passage we want to consider is an occasion where the apostle Peter went to a home of a man named Cornelius. A large group of people gathered at Cornelius' home. Peter began to preach to them about how God anointed Jesus with the Holy Spirit and power.

Luke, the author of the Book of Acts writes: "While Peter was still speaking these words, the Holy Spirit came on all who heard the message" (Acts 10:44).

We know something dramatic happened because the circumcised believers who had come with Peter were astonished that the gift of the Holy Spirit had been poured out on the Gentiles in Cornelius' house. These non-Jews responded to Peter's gospel message in the same way that the Jews who heard Peter preaching on the day of Pentecost responded as many became believers in Jesus Christ. They were born again of the Spirit, and then something else happened to them.

They were all filled with the Holy Spirit and, like those at Pentecost, began to speak in tongues and praise God. These new believers began to speak in unknown languages. Then Peter said, "Surely no one can stand in the way

PAY ATTENTION TO YOUR SPIRITUAL LIFE

of their being baptized with water? They have received the Holy Spirit just as we have. So he ordered that they be baptized in the name of Jesus Christ" (Acts 10:47–48).

This passage is clear evidence that the baptism in the Holy Spirit is most often a separate experience from conversion and water baptism. It is possible for one to be filled with the Spirit at their conversion or at the occasion of their water baptism, but the norm in the book of Acts seems to be that receiving this promise of the Father is a separate experience.

I know many people (including myself) who were baptized in water as an infant or later on as a youth or adult who then experienced the baptism with the Holy Spirit. I will share my experience later on.

In chapters 10 and 11 of Acts, Peter is relaying to the Jerusalem apostles how the Lord had shown him in a dream to kill and eat animals considered unclean by the Jews. Some men stopped at a house at which Peter was staying. These men asked Peter to go with them to the house of Cornelius, a Roman Centurion, to speak to the people in the house. Since Cornelius was a God-fearing Gentile on the path to becoming a Jew, Peter might have avoided eating with him and others in the house. He had a vision in which the Lord told him to kill and eat animals that were forbidden by Jews to eat. The Lord told him not to call anything unclean that He calls clean. In other words, Jesus was giving Peter permission to associate with Gentiles and to eat food that he once considered unclean. Peter then explained what had happened to him and the Gentiles at Cornelius' house. Peter said,

> As I began to speak, the Holy Spirit came on them as he had come on us at the beginning. Then I remembered what the Lord had said: "John baptized with water, but you will be baptized with the Holy Spirit."
> **Acts 11:15–16**

As we read one chapter earlier, when the Holy Spirit was poured out on these Gentiles, they began speaking in tongues and praising God.

It is interesting to note that this saying of John the Baptist (to be baptized with the Holy Spirit) is found in all four Gospels. It is found in Matthew 3:11, Mark 1:7–8, Luke 3:16, and John 1:33. These are the only references in each of these Gospel writings to the baptism with or in the Holy Spirit. Nowhere else in the four is the term baptism with the Spirit used nor is it explained anywhere within the chapters of these canonical writings.

The first reference outside of the Gospels of the phrase baptism with the Holy Spirit is found in Acts,

PAY ATTENTION TO YOUR SPIRITUAL LIFE

In my former book, Theophilus, I wrote about all that Jesus began to do and to teach until the day he was taken up to heaven, after giving instructions through the Holy Spirit to the apostles he had chosen. After his suffering, he presented himself to them and gave many convincing proofs that he was alive. He appeared to them over a period of forty days and spoke about the kingdom of God. On one occasion, while he was eating with them, he gave them this command: "Do not leave Jerusalem, but wait for the gift my Father promised, which you have heard me speak about. For John baptized with water, but in a few days, you will be baptized with the Holy Spirit."

Acts 1:1–5

Again, the phrase is not explained, but it points to a future event. That event is the day of Pentecost, where we find out the meaning of the phrase baptism with the Holy Spirit. The other passages I have noted above give further definition to this baptism with the Holy Spirit.

Returning now to St. Peter's explanation of the baptism with the Holy Spirit that happened in Cornelius' house, Peter explains to the Jerusalem Christians, "So if God gave them the same gift he gave us who believed in the Lord Jesus Christ, who was I to think that I could stand in God's way?" (Acts 11:17).

PAY ATTENTION

When the Spirit was poured out on the day of Pentecost, those believers may have thought that this experience was just for Jews. Peter thought the same way until he had a vision from God that he understood was God saying that all people in the world were to have the gospel preached to them allowing those who responded to the gospel message to become Christians. Before this vision (in Acts 10), Peter must have thought that the baptism in the Holy Spirit he and his fellow Jews had received was reserved only for those who he understood were children of Abraham.

Once he had seen what had happened to the Gentiles in Cornelius' home, he realized that God shows no partiality when it comes to salvation and the baptism in the Holy Spirit.

There is one last passage in Acts that refers specifically to the baptism in the Holy Spirit. In Acts 19, Paul was traveling to Ephesus. This was one of the places a Christian named Apollos went to preach. While Apollos did not know the fullness of the gospel, Luke says in Acts 18 Apollos taught about Jesus accurately. We can take from this that his preaching and teaching resulted in some people coming to put their faith in Jesus. These new Christians were no doubt eager to learn more about the faith they embraced.

When Paul arrived in Ephesus, he found these believers and asked them, "Did you receive the Holy Spirit when (or

PAY ATTENTION TO YOUR SPIRITUAL LIFE

after) you believed?" (Acts 2:19). Paul would have known that when one believes in Jesus the Holy Spirit comes to live inside of the believer. So, what did He mean by this question?

He meant, "have you received the power of the Holy Spirit since you have believed?"

Perhaps Apollos' teaching failed to tell them that when they believe in Jesus they are born again of the Spirit. He may not have explained that the Holy Spirit is sent by the Father into the believer.

Apollos may not have even mentioned the Holy Spirit, since he only knew about John the Baptist's baptismal formula.

The people responded to Paul's question about receiving the Spirit by saying,

> "No, we have not even heard that there is a Holy Spirit." So Paul asked, "Then what baptism did you receive?" "John's baptism," they replied. Paul said, "John's baptism was a baptism of repentance. He told the people to believe in the one coming after him, that is, in Jesus." On hearing this, they were baptized in the name of the Lord Jesus. When Paul placed his hands on them, the Holy Spirit came on them, and they spoke in tongues and prophesied. There were about twelve men in all.
>
> **Acts 19:2–7**

PAY ATTENTION

These Gentile believers in Jesus (who had the Holy Spirit living inside of them) were then properly baptized into Jesus Christ. Paul probably used the traditional baptismal formula (in the name of the Father, the Son, and the Holy Spirit).

After they were baptized in water, Paul placed his hands on them and they were all baptized in the Holy Spirit. "...the Holy Spirit came on them, and they spoke in tongues and prophesied" (Acts 19:6).

This is, yet again, another example of believers being baptized in the Holy Spirit after they believed and received water baptism.

Throughout the book of Acts we see the apostles and disciples of Jesus relying upon the power of this baptism in the Holy Spirit to do the things Jesus called them to do. Perhaps they had been taught the words of Jesus in John 14:12, "Very truly I tell you, whoever believes in me will do the works I have been doing, and they will do even greater things than these, because I am going to the Father."

Not only were the apostles and disciples doing miracles, casting out demons and healing people, they were often utilizing the other gifts of the Spirit as they ministered in Jesus' name.

As we have looked at various passages of Scripture

that speak about the baptism with or in the Holy Spirit, it is important to not make this simply a history lesson or intellectual exercise.

We must find out if this experience is still available today for the modern Christian. If it is still available, then how is one filled or baptized with the Holy Spirit?

One passage that can be helpful is found in Hebrews 13:8. "Jesus Christ is the same yesterday and today and forever." Jesus promised to give salvation to anyone who came to Him and made Him their Savior and Lord. Jesus rose from the dead showing that the promise of salvation is available to all today just as it was when He made the promise.

If Jesus is able to give salvation to people today as He did in the past, then there is no reason why He would or could not still baptize believers with the Holy Spirit.

Experience is another reason to believe that the baptism with the Holy Spirit is still available today. While experience alone is no proof of the reality of this baptism, experience plus Scripture give us more evidence of God continuing to fill the followers of Jesus. There are accounts throughout the Christian centuries of people being filled with the Holy Spirit. Although in most accounts in history the phrase baptized with the Holy Spirit is not used, the evidence of this baptism is seen in references to one of the gifts of the Spirit manifested in Christians throughout early church history up through the present day.

Irenaeus, who lived from 130 to 202 A.D., was a disciple of Polycarp who was in turn a pupil of the Apostle John. Irenaeus wrote in his book *Against Heresies*,

> In like manner do we also hear many brethren in the Church who possess prophetic gifts, and who through the Spirit speak all kinds of language and bring to light for the general benefit the hidden things of men and declare the mysteries of God, whom also the apostles term spiritual.
>
> **Irenaeus, (1981, 289)**

Tertullian, who lived about the same time as Irenaeus in 160–220 A.D., writes a passage in his book *Against Marcion* which challenges Marcion to produce anything among his followers such as was common among Tertullian's.

> Let him exhibit prophets such as have spoken, not by human sense but with the Spirit of God, such as have predicted things to come, and have made manifest the secrets of the heart; let him produce a psalm, a vision, a prayer, only let it be by the Spirit in an ecstasy, that is, in a rapture, whenever an interpretation of tongues has occurred to him.
>
> **Tertullian (1885, 445–447)**

PAY ATTENTION TO YOUR SPIRITUAL LIFE

A few years later in the third century, a certain Pachomius "after seasons of special prayer, spoke the Greek and Latin languages, which he had never learned, under the power of the Spirit" (Brumback, 1947, 91).

Saint Augustine, who lived in the fourth century (354–430) also wrote: "We still do what the apostles did when they laid hands on the Samaritans and called down the Holy Spirit on them by the laying on of hands. It is expected that converts should speak with new tongues" (Sherril, 1964, 76).

From the patristic times (the early church fathers) until the Protestant Reformation in the 1500s, the gift of tongues is an almost forgotten phenomenon. The attention which the Reformation drew to the Scripture is the reason for the reappearance of mention of the gifts of the Spirit along with the baptism with the Holy Spirit. Alexander Mackie, commenting on this disappearance and reappearance said, "Men do not usually have the gift of tongues unless they know there is a gift of tongues" (Mackie, 1950).

In a German work, Sourer's History of the Christian Church, it is stated that, Dr. Martin Luther was a prophet, evangelist, speaker in tongues, and interpreter, in one person, endowed with all the gifts of the Holy Spirit. (Brumback, 1961, 20).

The Encyclopedia Britannica tells of tongues "among

the converts of Wesley and Whitefield." Anglican John Wesley once wrote a protest against a Dr. Middleton who wrote "after the Apostolic time, there is not, in all history, one instance…of any person who had even exercised that gift (tongues)." Wesley replied, "Sir, your memory fails you again, it has been heard more than once no further off than the valleys of Dauphiny" (Brumback, 1947, 92).

The atmosphere of the revivals that followed the Wesleyan movement was one of informality, spiritual fervor, and religious enthusiasm. Crying out with groans and sobs in prayer, shouting and uttering "unintelligible sounds" were common of this early period" (Kendrick, 1961, 23).

A major reappearance of the baptism with the Holy Spirit and the manifestation of the gifts of the Spirit is seen with the revivals in Topeka, Kansas and Azuza Street in Los Angeles, CA. in the early 1900s. From these locations the message of the outpouring of the Holy Spirit was spread all over the world.

The Anglican clergyman Alexander A. Boddy in 1907 established his All Saints Church in Sunderland, England, as a Pentecostal center from which the movement of the Spirit spread throughout the British Isles.

Back in the United States the flames of revival in the liturgical churches began in the Episcopal church mainly through the ministry of Dennis Bennett, an Episcopal

PAY ATTENTION TO YOUR SPIRITUAL LIFE

priest in Van Nuys, California in 1960. Bennett has been credited with initiating the growing charismatic movement in the Episcopal/Anglican tradition. The late 60s also saw the movement beginning to touch the Roman Catholic church.

The evidence mentioned above seem to indicate that the Holy Spirit has been moving throughout Christian history. Many individuals in modern times have testified to being transformed by the power of the Spirit.

My story is one such testimony.

The earliest memory I have of church was when I was baptized in Grace Episcopal Church in Dallas at the age of seven. While I remember my baptism, I don't remember any real connection to Jesus until my parents sent me to a Vacation Bible School at a Baptist church. I remember watching a movie about Stephen the first recorded martyr of the New Testament church. I was amazed that someone would give up their life for their belief in Jesus. When the leader asked if any children wanted to give their life to Jesus, I raised my hand and prayed a prayer to accept Jesus. I don't remember if I felt anything other than a realization that something happened to me.

My parents took me to church regularly after that. I became an acolyte and offered to serve at the altar every Sunday. After church one Sunday a woman came up to me and said, "You are going to make a great priest someday." She probably didn't realize it, but she was prophesying something which would one day come to pass.

During my junior high years my parents began to have marital problems which meant that we rarely went to church. I began to drift away from the faith that was once a regular part of my life. During high school, I paid little attention to my spiritual life. In fact, I began to get involved in activities and friendships that would lead me further away from the Lord.

My best friend and I began to get involved with cannabis, even going so far as to be a local distributer for friends. This continued through my first year at Texas Tech University. I was seeking fulfillment through the pursuit of experiences and pleasures. During this time, I felt very empty and began to neglect my schoolwork. It became so bad that I was failing many of my classes during the first semester of my sophomore year. Since my father was paying for my education, I was terrified of what would happen if I failed my classes.

When finals came around, I needed to pass most of them and make an A on one of them to pass. I studied hard the night before my finals and made a desperate plea to God. I said, "If you will help me pass finals and get an A on the one I need, I will go to church." I hadn't been to church since well before I entered college.

PAY ATTENTION TO YOUR SPIRITUAL LIFE

It must have been a miracle, because not only did I pass all of my finals, I also got the A I needed. I was amazed and thankful. So much so, I realized that I had made the promise to go to church.

Because I was in college, I didn't want to get up on Sunday morning to go to church. I wondered if there was another way around this promise I had made. I came across a notice on a bulletin board near one of my classes. The notice advertised something called the Episcopal campus ministry which met on Sunday nights. I thought, *Hey, I'm Episcopalian, and this sounds kind of like church. Maybe I'll give it a try.*

The next Sunday night I went to the meeting not knowing what to expect. My experience with church was one of obligation more than enjoyment. I didn't expect this group to be much different than a regular church service. At least, I figured, there would be people my age there rather than mainly gray hairs I remember being the majority in churches of the past.

I met the Rev. Charles Pedersen, the priest in charge of this Episcopal campus ministry. He began to introduce me to the other students who had come. As I began to get to know them, many were unlike my usual opinion of a Christian. These were young people who were very committed to what they referred to their Lord Jesus.

PAY ATTENTION

Pedersen would often teach on the Holy Spirit. The group would sing contemporary songs of praise and thanksgiving. They seemed to have a belief in and love for Jesus that I didn't. They also showed the love of Jesus to me. These were not like the regular students at the university I had encountered. Although they were students like me, they seemed a lot less focused on themselves, less selfish than I was.

As I continued to attend, I learned that many of them had received what Pedersen called the baptism of the Holy Spirit. The more I attended, the more I wanted what he and these students had.

I met a guy in the group who was looking for a roommate. I was also looking to get out of the dorm in which I had been living. We decided to move in to an off-campus apartment the next September.

That fall, Steven, my roommate began to talk to me about his experience with the Holy Spirit. He talked about speaking in tongues, prophecy and other gifts of the Spirit. I pretended that I knew what he was talking about. He told me his father was an Episcopal priest who was head of the Episcopal Charismatic Fellowship. Charismatic. What was that? Again, even though I pretended to know what he was talking about, he eventually explained what charismatic meant. He said that an Episcopal charismatic was

PAY ATTENTION TO YOUR SPIRITUAL LIFE

someone in the Episcopal church who believed in (and has received) the baptism with the Holy Spirit.

I think Steven realized that I had not yet been baptized with the Holy Spirit, so he continued to teach me in more detail about what he had experienced. He also took me to various prayer meetings where people were prayed for to receive this baptism with the Spirit.

I received prayer to be filled with the Holy Spirit at several of these prayer meetings, but I felt like nothing happened. I continued to seek and pray for this baptism.

At the end of the fall semester, I went home for Christmas break. My parents were having major problems and were constantly arguing. It was a very tense time at home.

Most of the time, I hibernated in my room and watched TV. As I was flipping across the channels one night, I came across a talk show called the 700 Club on which the host was interviewing an Episcopal priest. I stopped and began to watch this interview. He gave his testimony about how he had paid attention to a couple in his church who were in the past simply regular members with not much involvement with the church outside of occasionally attending Sunday services.

One Sunday he began to notice something different about them They began to attend regularly, they volunteered to help in various areas of the church's ministry and they began to *tithe*. This was a shock to him, and he wondered what had happen to them. Why had they become so joyful, so full of life, so, well, helpful?

He met with them, and they told him of receiving the baptism with the Holy Spirit. Soon, this priest, Father Dennis Bennett, would receive the infilling of the Holy Spirit. He explained how his life was radically changed for the better after receiving this experience.

As he shared his testimony, I began to feel something happening within me. When he concluded, he asked if he could lead a prayer for those who were viewing this interview who wanted to receive the baptism with the Holy Spirit.

As he prayed, he asked to Lord to pour His love into the hearts of the viewers. As he prayed, I felt what I can only describe as liquid love pouring over me. I felt a joy that I had never felt before. Suddenly, Jesus became a real person to me rather than someone far off in heaven.

Father Bennett encouraged the viewers to begin to praise God, but not in English. I began to praise God and as I began to speak, I began speaking in what I would later come to understand as the gift of tongues. It flowed so naturally and effortlessly. I wondered if I could stop. I could, and I did. Then I wondered if I could start again. I could, and I did.

PAY ATTENTION TO YOUR SPIRITUAL LIFE

This deep experience of closeness with the Lord Jesus and His Spirit lasted for a number of weeks. It so transformed my life and my faith that I would never be the same. I began to read and understand the Bible for the first time. I began to pray often and regularly. It seemed so easy and so right. I felt like I was connecting with God in a way I had never been able to do before. I had a new desire to do what God wanted me to do and to follow Jesus to the best of my ability. I had a new power to pray for and share my faith with others.

From that time on, I was filled with a love and compassion for others that helped me to care for them, even bringing some into the kingdom of God.

I had such a hunger for the Word of God that I wanted to learn more about it and what it says. As I was about to graduate from Texas Tech with a degree in journalism, I realized that I no longer wanted to be in that field. I had discovered that to be a journalist, one had to compromise one's values, sensationalize stories and even fudge the truth a bit in order to get something published in the newspaper.

My new faith and walk with the Lord were leading me in a different direction. A friend of mine told me he was going out to attend a new startup seminary that was formed to equip and train people in order to send them back into their own denominations.

PAY ATTENTION

I had felt what I believed to be a calling from God to help bring this experience of the Holy Spirit to the Episcopal church. Pedersen had seen my growth in the Lord and we had talked about me becoming an Episcopal priest. He set up a meeting with the bishop of the Diocese of Northwest Texas. That bishop told me he didn't have any room for me at that time, but I should come back in a year or two.

I didn't particularly want to wait that long. So, when my friend told me about this new start up seminary, I decided that since I wanted to learn more about the Bible and to become an Episcopal priest, that I would attend in the fall.

The seminary, originally called Melodyland School of Theology. The name Melodyland was from the old Melodyland Theatre owned by Disneyland. These facilities (across the street from the theme park) were purchased by a church. The seminary that met at these facilities (made up of faculty from many different denominations) was designed to teach people solid theology along with how to minister in the power of the Holy Spirit.

I learned much during my time at Melodyland. I experienced many answers to prayer and had various gifts of the Spirit given to me for the benefit of others. I was even more inspired to bring the message of Jesus Christ and the baptism with the Holy Spirit to the Episcopal Church.

While I was at Melodyland, I found Trinity Episco-

PAY ATTENTION TO YOUR SPIRITUAL LIFE

pal Church in Orange, California. This church was open to the movement of the Holy Spirit. I began to do my seminary's required field work there. While at Trinity, I helped lead Life in the Spirit seminars and Youth Encounter Spirit weekends.

On one of those Life in the Spirit seminars, I remember a man in our congregation who was a very rough and gruff man. He was not a happy person. Somehow, he was talked into attending the seminar. He made it known that he was not at all interested in "this Holy Spirit stuff."

He paid little attention to his spiritual life until the fifth night of the seminar, when the Holy Spirit touched him. He not only committed his life to Christ but was marvelously filled with the Holy Spirit.

His whole life changed, he became the most loving man. He became an active member of the church and his family was so happy at this change in his life. He became a better husband, father, and Christian all because through the Holy Spirit, he began to pay attention to Jesus and his spiritual life.

When I graduated from Melodyland with a master of divinity degree, I continued to work at Trinity until eventually the rector of my church contacted Bishop Victor Rivera in the Diocese of San Joaquin who agreed to take me on as a postulant for holy orders (ordination). He required that

PAY ATTENTION

I attend another year of seminary at an Episcopal seminary after which I was ordained as a deacon and then eventually as a priest.

All of this came about because I paid attention at various times to what I believe was the leading of the Holy Spirit. The journey to ordination was not an easy one, nor was it always free of obstacles, seeming setbacks, and disappointments.

When you seek to pay attention to your spiritual life, seek to draw closer to Jesus and open yourself up to the Holy Spirit, God will lead you into His perfect will and plan. Just as Jesus paid attention to His spiritual life, drew close to His Father in heaven and was open to the leading of the Holy Spirit, he fulfilled the will of God and accomplished the plan of God set out for him. It wasn't easy. It was full of obstacles and setbacks. He faced opposition, criticism, and disappointment.

If he faced all of these things because he was full of the Holy Spirit, we should expect to face difficulties, challenges and obstacles as we seek to follow Jesus, and are filled with and walk in His Spirit.

The book of Hebrews articulates this well,

> Therefore, since we are surrounded by such a great cloud of witnesses, let us throw off ev-

PAY ATTENTION TO YOUR SPIRITUAL LIFE

erything that hinders and the sin that so easily entangles. And let us run with perseverance the race marked out for us, fixing our eyes on Jesus, the pioneer and perfecter of faith. For the joy set before him he endured the cross, scorning its shame, and sat down at the right hand of the throne of God. Consider him who endured such opposition from sinners, so that you will not grow weary and lose heart.

Hebrew 12:1–3

When we pay attention to Jesus through the Holy Spirit, walking in that Spirit, we will be led into the perfect will and plan of God. There is great joy when we know we are in a close relationship with Jesus through His Spirit. We begin to see God at work in us, around us, and through us. Though we face difficult times, challenges and disappointments, as we fix our spiritual eyes on Jesus we know that God will ultimately work out all things for our greatest good (Romans 8:28).

PAY ATTENTION TO THE VOICE OF GOD

Blondes have been the brunt of jokes for decades. Although this could be a joke about a brunette or redhead, I heard about a blonde who wanted to go ice fishing.

> She'd read many books on the subject. Finally, after getting all the necessary "tools" together, she made for the nearest frozen lake. After positioning her comfy stool, she started to make a circular cut in the ice. Suddenly, from the sky, a voice boomed, *"There are no fish under the ice!"* Startled, the blonde moved further down the ice, poured a Thermos of cappuccino and began to cut another hole in the ice. Again, from the heavens, the voice bellowed, *"There are no fish under the ice!"* The blonde, now quite worried, moved down to the opposite end of the ice, set up her stool, and tried again to cut her hole in the ice. The voice came once more, *"For the last time, there are no fish under the ice!"*
>
> She stopped, looked skyward, and said, "Is that you, Lord?"
>
> The voice replied, "No, you idiot! This is the ice rink manager." (No fish, 2000).

PAY ATTENTION

God wants to speak to us, but sometimes we don't recognize the voice of God, or we confuse other voices for the voice of God. Hearing God speak is not often easy, but recognizing God speaking to us and then paying attention to what He says can be even more challenging.

Once we learn to discern God's voice and separate His voice from other voices we might hear, we can begin to walk in a more intimate relationship with the Lord and walk in harmony and obedience to the God who speaks.

Once a person comes into a living relationship with Jesus Christ that person has access to God. Paul says in Ephesians 2:18 "For through him [Jesus] we both have access to the Father by one Spirit." When we receive Jesus Christ into our hearts and lives, the Holy Spirit comes to live inside of us. The Spirit gives us access to the Father which means that just as the Father spoke to Jesus through the Spirit, the Father also wants to speak to us through the Holy Spirit.

The Father speaks in different ways to people. He wants to speak to His children. Since believers in Jesus are described as children of God, it would make sense that the Father would want to speak to them. So, how does the Father speak to His children?

Jesus gives us a clue in John's Gospel,

PAY ATTENTION TO THE VOICE OF GOD

> But when he, the Spirit of truth, comes, he will guide you into all the truth; for He will not speak on His own; he will speak only what he hears, he will speak; and he will tell you what is to come.
>
> **John 16:13**

The Father speaks to His children through His Son Jesus. Jesus said on one occasion, "My sheep listen to my voice; I know them, and they follow me" (John 10:27). The writer to the Hebrews says this in chapter 1:1–2, "In the past God spoke to our ancestors through the prophets at many times and in various ways, but in these last days he has spoken to us by his Son…"

The Father speaks to us through Jesus. But Jesus is not just the mouthpiece of the Father, but the Son wants to speak to us as well.

There are many verses that indicate that Jesus speaks to His followers. Just as Jesus spoke to those who witnessed Him personally, so too, Jesus wants to speak to those who experience Him through a personal relationship with the Savior.

Jesus said He would speak to us. Since He will not be with us physically, how will He speak to us? He will speak to us through His Spirit,

> I have much more to say to you, more than you can now bear. But when He, the Spirit of truth,

> comes, he will guide you into all the truth. He will not speak on His own; he will speak only what he hears, and he will tell you what is yet to come.
> **John 16:12–13**

So, Jesus promises to speak to His followers. He will speak to them through the Holy Spirit. The Spirit speaks the true words of the Father and Jesus Christ.

Does the Holy Spirit speak on His own to us? According to the verse above, the Spirit only speaks what He hears from the Father and the Son. And yet, it is the Spirit's voice to which we must pay attention.

Now that we have determined that the Father and the Son want to speak to us through the Spirit, how do we hear, know, and recognize the voice of the Spirit?

In order to hear we must have *listening ears*. Jesus speaks of those who have "ears to hear" (Matthew 11:15; Mark 4:9). I remember as a kid there was a time that I didn't want to listen to something my brother was saying to me. So, I put my fingers in my ears and went "la la la" over and over again. That way I wouldn't have to listen to him.

While we may not put our fingers in our ears, many times, even as Christians, we don't want to listen to what God might be saying to us. For example, if God were to say to us that we need to forgive a certain person, do we ignore that clear word from God? We would recognize this

PAY ATTENTION TO THE VOICE OF GOD

as God speaking to us because it is in line with the words of Jesus. "But if you do not forgive others their sins, your Father will not forgive your sins" (Matthew 6:15).

We can develop a listening ear by first determining that we want to hear what God says to us, then beginning to practice listening. Many have found writing down what they believe God is saying to them to be particularly helpful.

Once we hear a word from God, then it is recumbent upon us to obey that word. We dare not try to change that word, or make it say something we want it to say but is contrary to what it really says.

When our daughter Elizabeth was starting to take ballet lessons, she had a number of leotards that would be used when she went to the dance studio.

One day, her mother saw Elizabeth dressed in a leotard. She wanted to go shopping and to take her daughter with her. She said, "go change your clothes so we can go shopping." Forty-five minutes later, Elizabeth came out still wearing a leotard. When her mother asked her why she had not changed, Elizabeth said, "I did, I changed into a different colored leotard." Elizabeth knew what her mother meant but didn't want to change into something besides a leotard. She listened to what her mother had said but ignored her mom's clear word.

As James puts it, "Do not merely listen to the word, and so deceive yourselves. Do what it says" (James 1:22).

More about this later.

What I am really talking about is learning how to pay attention to God when He speaks to us. Having determined that we want to hear and obey God's word, then the questions become "how does God speak to me?" and "how do I recognize His voice?"

There are eight main ways that God speaks to us. Some of these we can easily recognize, others may take some time to learn.

The main way that God speaks to us is through His word, the Bible.

Paul writes in 2 Timothy 3:16: "All Scripture is God-breathed and is useful for teaching, rebuking, correcting and training in righteousness," reminding us that God has spoken to us through the inspired words of the writers of Holy Scripture. These words are the main way that God teaches us what we need to know about His ways and will. They point out ways we have gotten off the track (rebuke). They help us to get back on the track (correcting) and they help us to learn what righteousness is (training) so that we can begin to live a more righteous life.

What you may not realize is that as you get into the Word of God and get the Word into you, God can begin to speak to you through His Word written.

When I was first filled with the Holy Spirit, I had a voracious appetite for the Bible. I read it a lot. I memorized

PAY ATTENTION TO THE VOICE OF GOD

various passages. I got to know God's Word through the help of the Holy Spirit.

I found that the Holy Spirit would often remind me of passages I had read and learned. I like this prayer in the Anglican Book of Common Prayer which underlines the importance of the Word of God,

> Blessed Lord, who caused all Holy Scriptures to be written for our learning: Grant us so to hear them, read, mark, learn, and inwardly digest them, that by patience and the comfort of your holy Word we may embrace and ever hold fast the blessed hope of everlasting life, which you have given us in our Savior Jesus Christ; who lives and reigns with you and the Holy Spirit, one God, for ever and ever. Amen
> **Anglican Church in North America (2019, 598)**

The prayer asks God's help so that we *"hear* them." Do you know that it is possible to hear something and not hear it? My wife can testify that sometimes she says something to me and realizes that I have not really heard her. We pray to *read*. Do you realize that this is a prayer that you can answer? By reading the Bible you get into the Word of God. We then pray to *mark* them. Now this doesn't mean that we have to mark up our Bibles. I make all sorts of notes and underlines in my Bible to highlight certain passages and thoughts. There is nothing wrong with marking up your

PAY ATTENTION

Bible if it is done to help you mark (pay attention) to what it is saying. We pray that we might *learn* the Scriptures. The only way to really learn the Scriptures is to study them. Think about the passages you read. Ask, "What is God trying to say through this passage and what is God trying to say *to me* through this passage?" Using the many available online commentaries and resources, we can not only gain a better understanding of God's word, but also to hide that word in our hearts so that we might not sin against God (Psalm 119:11).

I have found that memorizing Scripture is very important. The Holy Spirit often brings back to my mind passages I have memorized in the past. Often God speaks to me through those passages. When I am teaching a class at church, the Holy Spirit will often remind me of a passage that is relevant to what I am teaching.

Finally, we pray that we *inwardly digest* the Word of God. "How sweet are your words to my taste, sweeter than honey to my mouth!" (Psalm 119:103). "When your words came, I ate them; they were my joy and my heart's delight, for I bear your name, Lord God Almighty" (Jeremiah 15:16). Internalizing the Word of God can bring much satisfaction to our spirits and souls.

The Holy Spirit can bring a passage of scripture to your mind in order for God to speak something to you that

PAY ATTENTION TO THE VOICE OF GOD

you need to hear.

Sometimes a married person says, "I have fallen in love with this person. We love each other so much. I feel God is leading me to leave my spouse and start this new relationship."

But God has made it clear. He has said, "You shall not commit adultery" (Exodus 20:14). We can be quite sure that God will not guide us to commit adultery.

The Holy Spirit can bring back to your remembrance passages that you have learned (inwardly digested). You might remember a verse I quoted earlier in which Jesus was speaking to His disciples. "But the Advocate, the Holy Spirit, whom the Father will send in my name, will teach you all things and will remind you of everything I have said to you" (John 14:26). This not only helps us to know how the apostles and other biblical writers could remember everything they would eventually write down in the form of books or letters we find in the New Testament, but also how we can remember certain things the Lord has spoken to us either through His Word or through His voice within us.

I remember a time when I was at home, and I heard a knock at the door. I went to see who was there only to find some Jehovah's Witnesses at the door. I began to challenge some of the beliefs they were sharing with me. One in particular had to do with the deity of Christ. They believe that Jesus is "a god" but not a part of the Trinity or the Godhead.

The Holy Spirit brought back to my mind several scripture passages which I had learned earlier. I then asked the Witnesses to look these passages up in their Bibles.

I had them look up John 1:1–14, Colossians 1:13–20; 2:9 and Hebrews 1:3. These verses that I had read, marked, learned, and inwardly digested came back to me through the leading of the Holy Spirit.

Even though the Jehovah's Witness Bibles have mistranslated these verses, I was still able to cause them to think about who Jesus really is. They soon beat a hasty retreat.

The apostle Peter writes "But in your hearts set apart Christ as Lord. Always be prepared to give an answer to everyone who asks you to give a reason for the hope that you have. But do this with gentleness and respect" (1 Peter 3:15). You have a better chance of answering the questions of skeptics, unbelievers, and those with false beliefs if you know the Word of God.

The Holy Spirit doesn't just bring passages to mind to answer challenges to the Christian faith. The Spirit sometimes brings scripture passages to mind to help us when we have fallen into sin or deviated from the path of righteousness.

I remember a time when a person turned against me in one of the churches in which I have served. She was on the governing board of our church and voted to hire me as the pastor of the church. Within a couple of years of me being there I appointed her as Senior Warden of the church.

I had always made it plain to the search committee that my desire was to seek to get the denomination of which we were a part (the Episcopal church) to change its views on subjects like the inspiration and authority of the Bible and its views on the subjects like human sexuality. The leadership of that denomination were calling Scripture simply words written by men and could easily be ignored, changed, or rewritten.

The first few years of my time at that church, I and our diocese tried to affect that change from within at bishop's meetings and General Conventions. When it became apparent that the national organization was not going to change, our diocese made the decision to begin the process of leaving the denomination. I began to lead my church into an examination of the issues in order to determine whether we would follow the direction the diocese was heading.

Ultimately, a large majority of the church members and leaders voted to leave the Episcopal church. This now

PAY ATTENTION

former Senior Warden turned against me and began to try to undermine my ministry.

I was very angry at her and felt betrayed. I did not feel like forgiving her. I wanted God to "bless her with a brick." Not my finest hour.

It was then that the Holy Spirit brought back to my memory a verse I had learned years earlier. "And when you stand praying, if you hold anything against anyone, forgive them, so that your Father in heaven may forgive you your sin" (Mark 11:25).

Gulp! I didn't want to hear or listen to that word. Yet, I knew that for my spiritual health and progress, I needed to forgive her. I didn't want to until the Holy Spirit reminded me of how much God had forgiven me. If God had forgiven me, who was I to put myself above God by not forgiving this woman.

I made the decision to forgive her and found a great relief. She no longer dominated my thoughts, no longer caused heartache within me. I began to realize that because she thought of the Bible as somewhat flawed and fallible document, she could not see things the way I saw and understood the Word of God.

God wants to speak to us through His Word, but we must be willing to read it, learn it, pay attention to it, and get it into our minds and hearts.

PAY ATTENTION TO THE VOICE OF GOD

So, God speaks to us through His Word written. The second way God speaks to us is through His Son Jesus. Jesus speaks to us mainly through the voice of our conscience or directly to our minds in what the Bible calls a still small voice.

We read about such a voice in 1 Kings,

> Then the LORD said, "Go out and stand on the mountain in the presence of the LORD, for the LORD is about to pass by." Then a great and powerful wind tore the mountains apart and shattered the rocks before the LORD, but the LORD was not in the wind. After the wind there was an earthquake, but the LORD was not in the earthquake. After the earthquake came a fire, but the Lord was not in the fire. And after the fire a gentle whisper [still small voice]. When Elijah heard it, he pulled his cloak over his face and went out and stood at the mouth of the cave. Then a voice said to him, "What are you doing here, Elijah?"
>
> **1 Kings 19:11–13**

We often want Jesus to speak to us in some audible or dramatic way. While some have testified that they believed they have heard Jesus speak to them audibly, that is rare. Most of the time when Jesus speaks it is in a quiet way. He does so either through the voice of our conscience or through thoughts or impressions in our minds. The

PAY ATTENTION

Holy Spirit and the Word of God can help us to recognize whether this is the voice of Jesus or simply our own human thoughts. The Bible also indicates that Satan can speak to us as well. The discernment of the Spirit can help us to identify and recognize that the enemy is trying to speak to us.

If I go into a room with a lot of people gathered and I begin to talk to someone, that person may begin to gossip about someone. I might feel like joining in that gossip. Maybe the voice within me tells me to gossip about that person we are discussing. The voice may be still and small, but when I examine the voice in light of God's Word, then I know to reject that voice. The Word of God commands us not to gossip (Romans 1:29). So, I know that Jesus has not spoken the words I heard. It may well have been the voice of the devil.

On the other hand, Jesus may speak to me in a still small voice telling me to go to someone who is standing alone at our coffee hour at church. He may be speaking to me to help this visitor to our church to feel loved and cared for by the Lord and His church. I might then go to that person and engage them in conversation seeking to share the love of Jesus. I might then introduce them to someone else so that they can make a connection with other church members.

PAY ATTENTION TO THE VOICE OF GOD

Mike and Cindy were radically touched by God at a meeting led by Bill Johnson and Randy Clark. They live in an Islamic country and are engaged in evangelizing the Muslims of that country, which is illegal. In one village in the interior, where they had ministered for some time and had gained the respect of the local people, an event happened that confused them. They had befriended the most educated person in the village, who was responsible for turning in anyone who converted from Islam. The Islamic leader had seen many healings occur when Mike and Cindy prayed.

> One night their phone rang. It was the Islamic leader calling for Mike and Cindy. She said her mother was extremely ill, so Mike offered to visit the house. The leader was reticent. Mike told her, "This isn't about our theology or whose religion is correct, this is about your mother's life."
>
> The leader agreed that they could come over. When they arrived, several other members of the family were present. Mike thought, *Lord, what a great time for You to reveal yourself to this Muslim family.* Mike and Cindy entered, laid hands on the mother, and prayed in Jesus' name, but nothing happened. They left the village the next day to drive about eight hours to a large city. On the way, their cell phone rang.

PAY ATTENTION

"Mike, after you left, my mother's condition took a turn for the worse. We had to take her to the city, to the hospital. My family is angry with me for allowing atheists to pray for her." Muslims consider Christians either atheists or polytheists.

Mike did not understand why the mother had not been healed. He was confused because instead of bringing this family to Christ, the incident appeared to harden them to the gospel. Then the Holy Spirit told him to drive to the city, go into the hospital, and pray again for this mother. He obeyed. This time the whole extended family was present, over forty people in the room and in the hallway. The mother was now in critical condition and was not expected to live. Mike laid his hands on her and prayed again in Jesus' name. He still does not know why the family allowed him to do so. This time God healed her almost instantly!

When Mike was on his way home, the Holy Spirit spoke to him that by not healing her the first time, more of her family saw the power of God in Jesus' name the second time. And in the extended family at the hospital, more strategic people were present who needed to see the miracle (Johnson and Clark, 2011, 233–34).

Paying attention to the voice of God can often bring one into amazing experiences. Jesus wants to speak to us

PAY ATTENTION TO THE VOICE OF GOD

and if we have ears to hear that still small voice, we might be surprised at what we hear the Lord say.

Another way God can speak to us is through nature and creation. Paul says in Romans 1:20 "For since the creation of the world God's invisible qualities—his eternal power and divine nature—have been clearly seen, being understood from what has been made, so that people are without excuse."

While this passage points to nature and creation as evidences for the existence of God through the intricacies, complexities, design, and beauty of what He has made, it also helps us to realize that God has spoken and can speak to us through His creation.

How? By observing the ant's strength to store up food all summer long, we learn about wisdom and industriousness. By studying the heavens, we understand more of God's greatness. And through planting and growing a garden, we witness miracles of death and rebirth. God designed and spoke them all into existence.

Barry McGuire, one of the original members of The New Christy Minstrels, who made the song *Eve of Destruction* popular in the 1960s, tells the story of when he worked on a fishing boat outside of San Pedro, CA. He was out fishing one day, manning the helm, when he saw a dolphin break the water and come near the boat. He loved

PAY ATTENTION

dolphins, so he told his buddy to come man the wheel while he went down to the front of the boat.

> I'm leaning over as far as I can, I wanna touch him, you know. Hug him, do something. And I can't reach him, cause it's too far down to the water. So, I ran into the galley and I got a dishtowel and tied a big knot in the end of it. And I ran back up to the front of the boat and I'm leaning out in front of me, and I'm holding onto the stay, and I'm leaning out as far as I can. And when the dolphin breaks water right in front of the boat, I took the dishtowel with the knot and [I say,] "Hey!" Gave him a whack. This old dolphin had never been whacked by a dish towel before, so he goes back under the water and I can see him down there 15, or 20 feet it's crystal clear. And comes out of the water and he's looking like, "what is that?" and looking at me and he goes back into the water. And he drops back under the boat, and comes right up in front of the boat again and I "Hey!" and I give him another whack.
>
> Well, he swims off, and [I think] "Aww I scared him away. Bummer." So I went back on the wheel and I'm sitting out there with my buddy and we're talking about dolphins and how beautiful they are. And while we're talking here comes about thirty dolphins. "Woah!" I'm back down with my towel. And I'm knocking dolphins left and right and they are all shuffling

PAY ATTENTION TO THE VOICE OF GOD

over each other, "hit me, hit me," I spent about the next thirty-forty minutes just whacking dolphins and screaming…

Pretty soon, they all started to break away… pretty soon there was just one dolphin left. Just one. And he stayed with the boat for a long time… I felt that was the first one… I gave him a final whack with the towel and he swam off…

I remember sitting on the front of the boat that afternoon watching them swim away. And something deep, deep down in my heart whispered to me. "See those dolphins, Barry? I made those dolphins just for your pleasure" (McGuire, 1975).

God can speak to us through His creation.

Another way God speaks to us is through others. God may use a friend, teacher, parent, or preacher to convey His message of truth to us. Their words may come as a warning, a blessing, or a prophetic truth about our lives. Whether we choose to hear or ignore it, depends on us. Do their words line up with Scripture? Will God confirm or affirm that truth in us?

In Proverbs 11:14, Solomon says, "Where there is no counsel, the people fall; But in the multitude of counselors there is safety" (NKJV). Sometimes we need the perspective of another mature Christian to help us discern

PAY ATTENTION

whether what we have heard is really from God.

We need to be careful not to depend solely on the words of another person or persons assuming God was speaking to us through them. Is the person who is speaking to us a mature Christian? Do they have our best interests at heart? Are they speaking out of love and compassion or condemnation and judgment?

People sometimes feel the need to straighten us out. Granted, we may need straightening out, but their attitude is not one of encouragement or seeking to build us up, only to tear us down.

God sometimes speaks to us by popping words into our minds. This is especially important in the area of spiritual gifts. For example, God may pop into our minds a word related to someone else for whom He wants to do something. This may be in the form of a word of knowledge (one of the gifts of the Holy Spirit).

We see an example of this in Acts 5 with the story of Ananias and Sapphira who had sold some property and had claimed to have given all of the money to the apostles. Peter had a word of knowledge from God that Ananias had lied about giving the whole amount.

Teresa Lusk tells of her experience with the word of knowledge.

> One day, a friend invited me over to her lovely home. When I arrived, she had a smile on her

> face, offered me a drink, and sat down to talk to me as if her day could not have been any better than what she was portraying. Within a few minutes of my arrival I "knew" that someone had been crying deeply in one particular area of her living room. I got up and said, "Has someone been crying right here?" I pointed to the exact place where this emotional pain had been poured out. She admitted that it was her. I didn't need to know that my friend had been crying, but the Lord wanted to shine the light on her pain, that she may find comfort. (Lusk, 2020)

The word of knowledge can sometimes come in the form of a sympathy pain. Brendyn was a city planner in Pennsylvania. During a healing service he felt he could not move his neck to the right. He could move it to the left, but when he tried to move it to the right he could not.

He asked if anyone at the meeting was having trouble with a stiff neck and turning their head. A woman with this condition came up to him. After a few short prayers she was able to move her head both ways and had complete freedom of movement (Brendyn, 2019).

God will sometimes speak to us by popping a picture in our minds. Pastor John Wimber relays the following experience.

> It was the end of a long day of ministry and I was exhausted. I had just completed a teaching

PAY ATTENTION

conference in Chicago and was flying off to another speaking engagement in New York. I was looking forward to the plane ride as a chance to relax for a few hours before plunging back into teaching. But it was not to be the quiet, uneventful trip I had hoped for. Shortly after takeoff, I pushed back the reclining seat and readjusted the seat belt, preparing to relax. My eyes wandered around the cabin, not looking at anything in particular. Seated across the aisle from me was a middle-aged man, a business man, to judge from his appearance, but there was nothing unusual or noteworthy about him. But in the split second that my eyes happened to be cast in his direction, I saw something that startled me. Written across his face in very clear and distinct letters I thought I saw the word "adultery." I blinked, rubbed my eyes, and looked again. It was still there. "Adultery." I was seeing it not with my eyes, but in my mind's eye. No one else on the plane, I am sure, saw it. It was the Spirit of God communicating to me. The fact that it was a spiritual phenomenon made it no less real. By now the man had become aware that I was looking at him ("gaping at him" might be a more accurate description). "What do you want?" he snapped. As he spoke, a woman's name came clearly to mind. This was more familiar to me; I had become accustomed to the Holy Spirit bringing things to my awareness through these kinds of promptings. Somewhat nervously, I leaned

PAY ATTENTION TO THE VOICE OF GOD

across the aisle and asked, "Does the name Jane [not her real name] mean anything to you?" His face turned ashen. "We've got to talk," he stammered. The plane we were on was a jumbo jet, the kind with a small upstairs cocktail lounge. As I followed him up the stairs to the lounge, I sensed the Spirit speaking to me yet again. "Tell him if he doesn't turn from his adultery, I'm going to take him." Terrific. All I had wanted was a nice, peaceful plane ride to New York. Now here I was, sitting in an airplane cocktail lounge with a man I had never seen before, whose name I didn't even know, about to tell him God was going to take his life if he didn't stop his affair with some woman. We sat down in strained silence. He looked at me suspiciously for a moment, then asked, "Who told you that name?" "God told me," I blurted out. I was too rattled to think of a way to ease into the topic more gracefully. "*God* told you?" He almost shouted the question, he was so shocked by what I had said. "Yes," I answered, taking a deep breath. "He also told me to tell you... that unless you turn from this adulterous relationship, he is going to take your life." I braced myself for what I was sure would be an angry, defensive reaction, but to my relief the instant I spoke to him, his defensiveness crumbled, and his heart melted. In a choked, desperate voice he asked me, "What should I do?" At last I was back on familiar ground. I explained to him what it meant to repent and trust Christ and invited him to pray with me. With hands folded and heads bowed, I began to lead him in a quiet prayer. "Oh God…" That was as far as I got. The conviction of sin that had built up inside him seemed virtually to explode. Bursting into tears, he cried out, "O *God*, I'm so *sorry*" and launched into the most heartrending repentance I had ever heard. It was impossible, in such cramped quarters, to keep hidden what was happening. Before long everyone in the cocktail lounge was intimately acquainted with this man's past sinfulness and present contrition. The flight attendants were even weeping right along with him. When he finished praying and regained his composure, we talked for a while about what had happened to him. "The reason I was so upset when you first mentioned that name to me," he explained, "was that my wife was sitting in the seat right next to me. I didn't want her to hear." I knew he wasn't going to like what I said to him next. "You're going to have to tell her." "I am?" he responded weakly. "When?" "Better do it right now," I said gently. The prospect of confessing to his wife was, understandably, somewhat intimidating, but he could see there was no other way. So again, I followed him, down the stairs and back to our seats. I couldn't hear the conversation over the noise of the plane, but I could see his wife's stunned reaction, not only to his confession of infidelity, but also to his account of how the stranger sitting across the aisle had been sent

PAY ATTENTION TO THE VOICE OF GOD

by God to warn him of the consequences of his sin. Eyes wide with amazement (and probably terror!), she stared first at her husband, then at me, then back at her husband, then back at me, as the amazing story unfolded. In the end the man led his wife to accept Christ, right there on the airplane. There was little time to talk when we got off the airplane in New York. They didn't own a Bible, so I gave them mine. Then we went our separate ways. (Wimber and Springer, 2009, 74).

Dreams can be a way that God might speak to us. Randy Clark shares about a time when he was in Uberlandia, Brazil ministering to a large church of several thousand members

> I was in Brazil and had a dream. I clearly saw two hands with long splinters stuck into them from the bottom of the index finger around the thumb area and then to the center of the palms. The splinters came all the way out two inches past the other side of the hand. I was not sure this was God, never having received a word in a dream. In a meeting, I gave the word last in case I was wrong. A man seated on the back row quickly came to the front. He put his outstretched hand in mine. Before I could pray a sentence he was healed. I could see the large scar exactly as I had described it. He had been in pain since the accident, and his hand had

been paralyzed in an open position. The pain and the paralysis ended a few seconds after he laid his hand in mine. (I am not sure why I saw two hands in the dream, whereas the man had injured only one. I was just glad to receive a word of knowledge that brought about his healing.) (Johnson and Clark, 2011, 147)

Another way God may speak to us is through music. Sometimes the lyrics of a song can be God speaking to you. I remember when I felt God calling me to go from Portland, OR to Buffalo, NY to accept a position in a church. They interviewed me in the summer when the weather was beautiful, but did not tell me about the winters. After three months of snow, I began to wonder if I had heard God's call to go to this snowy region. I was listening to an album entitled *To the Bride* which had a song called "I Walked a Mile." God spoke to me through the chorus of that song. The chorus went like this "Blessed are you when you trust, what you just can't understand" (Mcguire, 2009). At that moment, I believe God was telling me that He had a plan and that I just needed to trust Him.

Over two years later, I came across an advertisement in a magazine called the Living Church. The ad was for a position in Fort Worth, TX at an Episcopal church. I applied and interviewed and received a call to become the Rector of St. Anne's Episcopal Church.

PAY ATTENTION TO THE VOICE OF GOD

I later found out that the church had called someone else to be the Rector, but he had turned them down. This caused the search committee to start looking again. That is when I came across the ad in the magazine.

I believe I would never have been called to this church in which I am now serving, if I had still been in Portland, OR. God's plan was to move me to a place which would be the next step to the place where I would find such love and encouragement, and where I could minister to people not far from where I was born (Dallas).

While there were many great people in New York, the diocese my church was in was very theologically liberal. I always felt like I was having to defend the faith once delivered to all the saints to a people who didn't want it defended. I didn't feel like this is where God wanted me long term. I was able to endure this transition period in New York partly because I was, as the song said, trusting God in the midst of a situation I did not understand.

God can not only use music with lyrics to speak to us, but, I have found that He can also speak to us through the beauty of instrumental music. I remember driving down the road one day. I had a vision of heaven and steps leading to the throne of God while I was listening to entirety of Elgar's Pomp and Circumstance. It was as if God were speaking to me, saying, "I'm preparing a home in heaven for you and here is a glimpse of my majesty."

As we have seen, God can speak to us in many different ways. Often when God speaks, He is seeking to guide us to do something, say something, go somewhere, see someone, or accomplish some aspect of His will for us.

The main ways God uses to guide us can be best understood using some teaching from the international Alpha Course. One of the leaders of Alpha in the U.K. is Nicky Gumbel. He has come up with five ways God guides using the letters C.S. Commanding Scripture, Compelling Spirit, the Counsel of the Saints, Common Sense, and Circumstantial Signs.

I have addressed the first three in the text above. As we pay attention to God speaking to us though Holy Scripture, we often find that God can guide us through the pages of Scripture (Commanding Scripture). We can see God guiding us through the leading of the Holy Spirit (Compelling Spirit). God can speak to us through our brothers and sisters in Christ (Counsel of the Saints).

So, how does Common Sense fit into hearing God's voice. God doesn't always need to speak to us about every little thing. He has given us a mind to think rationally. The Bible will often tell us the general will of God. We know from Scripture, for example, that singleness is a high calling affording a single person an opportunity to draw closer

PAY ATTENTION TO THE VOICE OF GOD

to God in a way that is more difficult for a married person (see 1 Corinthians 7:25–39).

While the Bible says that marriage is the norm, it does not tell one whom he should marry. Common sense tells us that we need not look to the Bible to tell us whom to marry. If I was a single woman, I wouldn't say, "I'm going to open up the Bible and point and the first name I come to will be the one that God wants me to marry." What if my finger lands on the name Abishag (I Kings 1:3,4; 2:13–25)? Not much chance of coming across an Abishag.

It's common sense. Am I compatible with that person? Are we spiritually in sync? Am I attracted to this person? Questions like these are common sense questions that God gave us a mind to come up with.

God can speak to us by using the common sense He gave us. Sometimes we might want to test our common sense by running our thoughts or ideas by a fellow Christian (Counsel of the Saints).

Circumstantial Signs can be another way that God can speak to us and guide us. God can even use supernatural manifestations to speak to us. In Scripture we read of God speaking through a burning bush and through a donkey.

As you begin to want to hear God speaking to you and as you begin to pay attention to the different ways He may speak to you, many adventures, life changing opportunities and even miracles will come your way.

God is working for your good. That's who He is. It is part of His nature. He can't help Himself. All that has happened to you, God can use for good. Your past mistakes, the bad and horrible, God can redeem and turn them to good. Nothing is beyond Him or His grace. In Romans 8:28 the apostle Paul says, "And we know that in all things God works for the good of those who love him and have been called according to his purpose."

As evidenced in some of the stories above, it is not enough just to hear God speak to us. We must also act on what we hear. The apostle James calls this being a "doer of the word." James 1:22 puts it this way "Do not merely listen to the word, and so deceive yourselves. Do what it says."

One of the hardest things for the Christian to do is to regularly obey the word of God. Whether it be the Word written giving some command to be obeyed or some word given to us by the Holy Spirit related to our speech, actions, or behavior.

Our sinful nature rises up within us and rebels against any attempt by someone (God) or something (His Word) to tell us what to do. Even though our spirits are redeemed by Christ, there is still a battle going on within us. It is not just a battle of good and evil, it is a battle of our selfish nature and our godly spiritual nature.

PAY ATTENTION TO THE VOICE OF GOD

Even the great apostle Paul struggled with this inner battle. He describes his struggles this way,

> We know that the law [God's commandments] is spiritual; but I am unspiritual, sold as a slave to sin. I do not understand what I do. For what I want to do I do not do, but what I hate I do. And if I do what I do not want to do, I agree that the law is good. As it is, it is no longer I myself who do it, but it is sin living in me. For I know that good itself does not dwell in me, that is, in my sinful nature. For I have the desire to do what is good, but I cannot carry it out. For I do not do the good I want to do, but the evil I do not want to do—this I keep on doing. Now if I do what I do not want to do, it is no longer I who do it, but it is sin living in me that does it.
> **Romans 7:14–24**

Paul is describing the inward battle that goes on in us. We have a dual nature living within us. When the Holy Spirit comes to live inside us through faith in Christ, the Spirit does not immediately take away all of our sinful desires and actions. God allows the sinful nature to remain in us until it is fully done away with when we get to heaven.

Jesus wants us to choose to live in obedience to Him and His commandments. This reminds us that we are not puppets being controlled by a divine puppet master. We have the freedom to choose to follow Jesus and His commandments.

PAY ATTENTION

The Holy Spirit is working in us throughout the rest of our lives to bring our wills, behaviors, and actions in line with God's will. The Spirit is working to transform our sinful nature into a more Christ-like nature.

Each human being has aspects of the nature of God within them. That is why even non-Christians can at times do good things, act and speak lovingly, and appear to be good people. That nature of God has been corrupted by sin and thus we all now have the propensity to be selfish and to give into our sinful nature.

The Holy Spirit is trying to restore within the life of the Christian those God-given qualities that humans were originally created to have. These qualities are called by St. Paul, the "fruit of the Spirit."

In Galatians 5 Paul describes the goal of the Christian life. We are to be free from the influence of the sinful nature. "You, my brothers and sisters, were called to be free. But do not use your freedom to indulge the flesh [sinful nature], rather serve one another humbly in love" (Galatians 5:13).

We are called to be free from following the desires of the flesh when those desires lead us away from the will and ways of God. How does one do this? How do we follow the commandments of God and not give into the sinful human nature?

PAY ATTENTION TO THE VOICE OF GOD

Paul suggests

> So, I say, walk by the Spirit, and you will not gratify the desires of the flesh. For the flesh desires what is contrary to the Spirit, and the Spirit what is contrary to the flesh. They are in conflict with each other, so that you are not to do whatever you want.
> **Galatians 5:16–17**

You might remember what God said He would do to His people. He said He would put His Spirit within them and move them to follow His decrees and be careful to keep His laws (Ezekiel 36:25–27). So, if we are walking by the Spirit (being led and guided by the Spirit), we will be walking in obedience to God's commands not by will power, but rather it will almost be second nature. The nature of the Spirit!

God spoke to Zechariah on one occasion: "So he said to me, 'This is the word of the Lord to Zerubbabel: Not by might nor by power, but by my Spirit,' says the Lord of Hosts" (Zechariah 4:6). As we yield ourselves to the voice and leading of the Holy Spirit, God gives us the power (and desire) to obey His commands.

Paul goes on in Ephesians 5 to describe the two natures resident within the Christian. The sinful human nature and the redeemed spiritual nature (influenced and led by the Holy Spirit).

PAY ATTENTION

He says the acts or fruit of the sinful human nature within us are obvious. Our desires within us to disobey God's commands, to be selfish and to walk in our own way apart from God's way are clearly seen in how we behave, think and speak. Left to its own devices, the flesh or sinful nature will sometimes move us to act in ways that are either wrong or not beneficial for ourselves or others. Paul lists some of those actions that are led by the flesh or sinful nature when he says, "The acts of the sinful nature are obvious: sexual immorality, impurity, and debauchery, idolatry, witchcraft; hatred, discord, jealousy, fits of rage, selfish ambition, dissensions, factions and envy; drunkenness, orgies, and the like" (Galatians 5:19–21).

Sexual immorality is any type of sexual activity outside of the biblically described marriage relationship. Impurity really includes all kinds of sin and encompasses any activity, thought, word, or action that does not conform to God's will for our lives. "God did not call us to be impure, but to live a holy life" (1 Thessalonians 4:7).

Debauchery is the habitual and unrestrained indulgence of lust and sensuality. It encompasses several aspects of unholy living, including but not limited to sexual immorality, drunkenness, crude talk, and generally out-of-control behavior. Idolatry is to place anything or anyone in the place of God as to worship that thing or person. Witch-

PAY ATTENTION TO THE VOICE OF GOD

craft includes many things like what is described in Deuteronomy 18:12, "Let no one be found among you who sacrifices their son or daughter in the fire." Could this be related to modern day abortion? The scripture continues, "who practices divination or sorcery, interprets omens, engages in witchcraft, or casts spells, or who is a medium or spiritist or who consults the dead. Anyone who does these things is detestable to the Lord" (Deuteronomy 18:10–12).

This verse also condemns drunkenness whether by alcohol or other substances, orgies, and "the like" meaning anything else he didn't mention that would be a fruit of the flesh or sinful nature.

Paul says that those who practice these things as a normal pattern in their life without any repentance or attempt to be led by the Spirit will not inherit the kingdom of God. In other words, those without Christ have no real desire to live by the commandments of God but rather their natural proclivity is to live by the flesh.

The Christian may succumb to aspects of the fruit of the flesh, but that will not be the normal pattern of their life. When they give into one of these sins, they will seek the forgiveness of God and the help of the Holy Spirit to forsake that sin and empower them to resist the temptation to give into that sin again. The Christian will not be conformed any longer to the pattern of this world but will

PAY ATTENTION

seek to be transformed by having their minds renewed to think more like Christ and His Word. They will do this so that they may know and accept what God's will is for their lives, "his good, pleasing and perfect will" (Romans 12:2).

The devil and his demons will always be seeking to take the believer's attention off of the Lord and what pleases Him and to focus on what the believer's sinful nature wants and what it will take to please that nature. The believer's sinful nature, however, does not need any help from the devil to disobey.

> Those who live according to the flesh have their minds set on what the flesh desires; but those who live in accordance with the Spirit have their minds set on what the Spirit desires. The mind governed by the flesh is death, but the mind governed by the Spirit is life and peace. The mind governed by the flesh is hostile to God; it does not submit to God's law, nor can it do so. Those who are in the realm of the flesh cannot please God.
> **Romans 8:5–8**

We might often wonder why unbelievers can't see the truth of God the way we believe we can. Paul says that those without the Holy Spirit living inside of them can't see these truths because they are spiritually discerned. "The person without the Spirit does not accept the things that come from the Spirit of God but considers them foolishness and cannot understand them because they are discerned only through the Spirit" (1 Corinthians 2:14).

As Paul says in Romans 8, unbelievers can't by nature regularly obey the laws of God, nor can they understand many things related to the Christian faith. God gives every unbeliever the ability to hear and understand the gospel in terms of receiving salvation, but when it comes to the deeper things of God, they often can't seem to understand them.

This is why we should not expect unbelievers to live like Christians are supposed to live. Since they don't have the Spirit, they just can't do it. We should never expect them to "clean up their act" before they come to faith in Christ. Since we are called to be fishers of people (Matthew 4:19), we catch the fish and Christ cleans the fish, not vice-versa.

The fruit or acts of the sinful nature are what the Holy Spirit is seeking to move the believer away from. The Spirit is trying to move the followers of Jesus towards righteousness. Paul describes that righteousness in terms of a different type of fruit. He calls that fruit the fruit of the Spirit. Things like love, joy, peace, patience, kindness, goodness, faithfulness, gentleness and self-control(Galatians 5:22–23).

PAY ATTENTION

If you think about these aspects of the fruit of the Spirit, you may realize that these are describing aspects of the nature of God. God possesses all of these qualities in perfection. He has given Christians the *image* of those qualities. These qualities were corrupted by sin and thus are not able to be lived out in their originally designed way.

Through Christ, those qualities of God have been energized and given new life. They are like developing fruit on a fruit tree. A tree's fruit starts out small but eventually grows to its full fruitfulness.

So, too, does the fruit of the Spirit start out relatively undeveloped and then begins to grow. It grows as the believer is submitted to Jesus and seeking to stay close or abide in Christ. He is the vine to which we are attached. If we abide or remain in Him, the fruit of the Spirit grows within us.

John quotes Jesus,

> I am the true vine, and my Father is the gardener. He cuts off every branch in me that bears no fruit, while every branch that does bear fruit he prunes so that it will be even more fruitful. You are already clean because of the word I have spoken to you. Remain in me, as I also remain in you. No branch can bear fruit by itself; it must remain in the vine. Neither can you bear fruit unless you remain in me. I am the vine;

PAY ATTENTION TO THE VOICE OF GOD

> you are the branches. If you remain in me and I in you, you will bear much fruit; apart from me you can do nothing.
>
> **John 15:1–5**

Not only are we to remain or abide in Christ, we are also to remain or abide in His Word. Christ and His Word will allow the Spirit to grow the fruit of righteousness within us.

Jesus said in John,

> If you remain in me and my words remain in you, ask whatever you wish, and it will be done for you. This is to my Father's glory, that you bear much fruit, showing yourselves to be my disciples. As the Father has loved me, so have I loved you. Now remain in my love. If you keep my commandments, you will remain in my love just as I have kept my Father's commands and remain in his love.
>
> **John 15:7–12**

This passage appears to say that if you remain in Jesus and His words then you can ask for anything and get it. In reality, if you remain in Jesus and His words, you won't be asking for anything that is not according to His will. God answers prayers that are according to His will (1 John 5:14).

A few years ago, a popular saying among Christians was "What Would Jesus Do?" abbreviated as WWJD. As

PAY ATTENTION

we remain or abide in Jesus we begin to think like Jesus. We begin to think of how Jesus might respond to a situation, a temptation or a relationship. The closer we are to Christ the better able we will be to walk in the Spirit. As we walk in the Spirit, we are giving permission to the Holy Spirit to transform, lead, and guide our human spirits in the right path: the path of righteousness.

As we pay attention to our relationship with Jesus and as we submit ourselves to the Holy Spirit, God begins to inspire us to behave, think and speak more like Jesus would behave, think and speak.

When we abide in Christ we become better able to hear His voice as He, the Father and the Spirit speak to us in the various ways mentioned above.

PAY ATTENTION TO YOUR FAMILY

When it comes to paying attention sometimes one of the most neglected parts of our lives is our family. We can become so self-focused that we don't pay much attention to our family. We can become so focused on our church life that we neglect our family. This can be especially true for the rector or pastor of a church as well as those lay people who are super dedicated to their ministries in the church.

Some who serve in the church find that they receive a lot of affirmation and satisfaction in their service. They want to spend more time at the place where they are affirmed or where they think they are making a difference.

The church certainly needs dedicated people to serve and minister in the name of Christ. The church also needs healthy people to serve. Spiritually healthy people know how to balance their church lives with their family lives.

There are two aspects of paying attention to family that I want to address.

First, is our relationship with our extended family. You may be a single person and you may be thinking that this chapter is really not for you.

Not so! If you have no parents or other relatives in

your life because they are deceased, then you will want to develop a new family. It is probably best that this family comes from your church as you may develop a caring, close-knit relationship with a few church members who could become a surrogate family.

I remember when I was single and living in Bakersfield, California, the church secretary and her husband began to take an interest in me, inviting me to dinner occasionally. The husband, Roy would invite me to go out golfing. Marie, his wife, would regularly check in with me to see how I was doing. They became a kind of family for me since my father had died many years earlier and my mother was in Oklahoma and thus, far away. I developed a close relationship with other people in the church and these relationships began to blossom into a kind of extended family. I would take an interest in their lives and seek to give them love and encouragement to build them up in their faith.

The church can become a real source of family not only for the single person, but also for those that are married.

When my wife and I lived in Portland, OR, I was serving as the Rector of St. Matthew's Episcopal Church. A couple in the church invited us over to dinner and we hit it off. This couple did little things that drew us closer to them, like inviting us over to their home for major holi-

PAY ATTENTION TO YOUR FAMILY

days. They became a sort of family. I had no family nearby and much of Nancy's family was down in California.

As the rector of the church, I had to be careful not to show favoritism towards this couple to the exclusion of the other parishioners. Sometimes parishioners want to get in good with the rector in order to wield some influence in church politics and decision making.

I never felt like this couple had such an agenda but were simply seeking to share the love of Christ with us.

If you have an extended family (parents, grandparents, aunts, uncles, nieces, nephews, etc.) in the town where you live (or nearby in a local community) it is important to pay attention to them. If they are not believers in Jesus, you have the opportunity to be an ambassador for Christ by seeking to be an example of the love of Christ in what you do and say. Witnessing to family is often one of the most difficult aspects of Christian witnessing.

As you pay attention to your extended family by keeping in regular contact with them, seeking ways to serve them, and sharing the love and joy of the Lord with them, then doors may open for you to share Christ with them. Even if that doesn't happen, they will have a much more favorable impression of Christianity because they see the sincerity, grace, and love with which you deal with them.

One of the things that can make a difference in your

PAY ATTENTION

extended family is to pray for them. You can also ask them if there might be something in their lives for which you can pray. By following up on that request, you show a real interest in their lives. This again will reflect the love of Christ, perhaps drawing them to faith in Jesus.

If your parents are still alive, pay attention to them. As adults age, children leave the home (most of the time) and the adults are left as empty nesters. This can be a great time for couples to rekindle a relationship that may have cooled off a bit because of the focus of raising children.

At the same time, parents may feel like their children no longer need or want them. I have seen many people in nursing homes who have rarely or never been visited by a son or daughter. In other situations, I have seen the children become the parents treating their parents like little children. They are constantly critical of their parents, often giving them unsolicited advice. Sometimes adult children take advantage of their parents financially. They can think that their parents have nothing to do but to cater to their whims. Parents can become a babysitting service rather than having occasional bonding times with the grandkids. Adult children can, at times, treat their parents the way they remember being treated by their parents as children.

While some parents want to continue to try to run their adult children's lives, most parents just want to know their

PAY ATTENTION TO YOUR FAMILY

kids are okay. They want to know some of the challenges that their children are facing so that they know how best to pray for them. Some parents can be great sounding boards as children ask for advice from the parents who have experienced much more of life. There can be a wisdom in many parents that can go untapped by their children.

We often love our parents so much that we want to make life easy for them. Does that sound familiar? We may want them to stop driving because we feel they are unsafe on the road. We may want them to move into a nursing home because we feel they are unable to care for themselves.

More than a few children have found navigating these treacherous waters to be stressful or seemingly impossible. This is especially true if their parents want to continue to hold on to things which they believe are tied to their independence.

Adult children can become angry and bitter at their parents whom they see as causing problems for them and their family. Some adult children, because of location, may feel like all of the responsibility is falling on them to the exclusion of their other siblings. Those siblings sometimes don't seem interesting in dealing with the issues facing their parents. Sometimes children who live far away from the parents don't really know how they can help or what they can do to take the burden off of the siblings who are having to deal with aging parents.

Taking care of an elderly or aging parent can be tough enough to begin with. However, when aging parents get mean, or when aging parents expect too much, it can even double the already existing stress. Maybe it's as simple as mom and dad just being a little stubborn about taking some of your financial or life advice, or maybe it's as complicated as giving up your life to care for an elderly parent, because of growing physical health concerns or cognitive impairment, such as dementia. You may even wonder if you are legally responsible for your elderly parents. Have asked yourself, "Am I responsible for my parent's debt after they die?" These are all good questions to ask and very valid concerns. One might want to consult an attorney or some other professional familiar with situations like this.

Look at what the apostle Paul says in 1 Timothy 5:3–4:

> Give proper recognition to those widows who are really in need. But if a widow has children or grandchildren, these should learn first of all to put their religion into practice by caring for their own family and so repaying their parents and grandparents, for this is pleasing to God. The widow who is really in need and left alone puts her hope in God and continues night and day to pray and ask God for help. But the widow who lives for pleasure is dead even while

PAY ATTENTION TO YOUR FAMILY

> she lives. Give the people these instructions, so that no one may be open to blame. Anyone who does not provide for their relatives, and especially for their own household, has denied the faith and is worse than an unbeliever.
>
> **1 Timothy 5:3–4**

Reading a passage like this, many children feel obliged to take care of their elderly parents as they age, but it can be a great burden, particularly if they still are raising children of their own and managing a full-time career and household. It often appears that daughters are more likely to take over the caretaker role than sons, so these daughters are adding to an already full plate as mom, wife, employee, possibly even student, homemaker, and now caretaker.

Many aging parents expect a level of full-time care that their children simply can't provide, and at the same time, don't want strangers, like nurses, home health aides, or hospice workers coming into the home. Many children want to be responsible for caring for elderly parents. The stress involved in doing this can be overwhelming, however. When caregivers begin to reach burnout, they start to wonder if they are legally and financially responsible for their parents, especially if their aging parents expect or require too much from them.

Aging parents can get to the place where they should no longer be driving a car. Their children face a tough choice as to whether to take away the car keys or not. Driving is the second hardest thing for a parent to give up. The first, of course, is the home in which they have lived in for an extended time.

There may be times when the best option for parent care is for them to go into a facility that is best equipped to handle their aging issues.

While there are no easy answers to these challenges, the Christian child will want to pay attention to their parents and have as their guiding principle, the fifth of the Ten Commandments. "Honor your father and your mother, so that you may live long in the land the Lord your God is giving you" (Exodus 20:12).

Are there ways that you are not honoring your parents? Perhaps you are being short with them, or you are taking advantage of them financially. Maybe you are just trying to pawn them off on someone else or an institution to get them out of your hair. Are you trying to force your ideas and advice on them?

Although it may be difficult, are we paying attention to our parents in the way God wants us to? Is God speaking to us about how we are to treat our parents? Some helpful scripture verses include 1 Timothy 5:4, 8, 16 and Proverbs 23:22.

What about parents and children (teens, adolescents,

PAY ATTENTION TO YOUR FAMILY

and youngsters) living under the same roof? In what ways are we to pay attention?

Let me address parents first. Pay attention to your children. This seems an obvious statement, and yet I have seen parents who are more concerned about their own happiness, comfort, schedule, and desires.

Most young children are starving for attention from their parents. They often act out to try to get their parent's attention. From "Dad, can we play a game together," to "Mom, can we go shopping together," kids want the attention of their parents.

My wife, daughters, and I were visiting another family at their lake house one Fourth of July. One of the family members had his young son Jim and daughter Wendy [names changed] with him. The father was lighting fireworks with his son. Wendy was on the swing nearby. She said, "Daddy, can you push me?"

My daughter, who was standing near the swing said, "I'll push you."

"No, I want Daddy to push me," she shouted. "Daddy, will you push me?"

Jim said, "Dad will you light this firework for me?" Dad was torn not knowing which one who needed his attention more. They both were longing for attention from their father.

PAY ATTENTION

How often do I look back on my children's lives growing up and regret the times I said when they asked to play or do something with them, "I'm too tired to play," or "I'm watching this TV show right now," or "Let me finish doing this stuff on the computer."

I remember the joy on the faces of my children when I paid just a little attention to them by playing a card game (Go Fish was one of our favorites) or a board game.

Even taking one of my daughters with me when I went shopping for something I needed made such a difference. I remember taking Alexandra to a shopping mall. As we were running in the rain to get to the mall, I was holding her hand and went too fast. I pulled her so hard she fell face first on the hard concrete. I felt horrible as we walked back to the car to go home to get her cleaned up and bandaged. I apologized profusely. She continued to say, "It's okay, Dad." She just appreciated that I was spending time with her.

How quickly they grow up and then you begin to realize you won't have the chance to give them the attention you now want to give.

Parents involved in a divorce situation realize the difficulty of giving the attention they want to give. Because one parent may not have custody, the non-custodial parent often goes overboard in trying to make up for not having

PAY ATTENTION TO YOUR FAMILY

the time to pay attention to their child. They may try to buy their children things as a way of *paying attention*. While the child may like what they have received, it doesn't compare to the personal attention that they crave from the parent.

The child may realize they are not going to get the attention from the parent that they want and resign themselves to playing alone with the toy that mom or dad purchased. It can get to the point where the child thinks, "I can't get my parent's attention, so I might as well try to get as many things out of the parent as possible. Maybe that will fill up the emptiness that I am feeling from the attention I am lacking."

Television, computers, computer games, and social media have become the norm for information and entertainment. We spend an amazing amount of time on our phones, tablets, and computers. These things can be beneficial, but they can also be a distraction keeping us from paying attention to what is important.

Children today have access to things online that would have been unthinkable even a decade ago. Many young people have ways of visiting websites that can shield their parents from seeing what they are doing.

Many children while online come across pornography, violence, and other graphic images that can negatively affect their still forming brains. Websites like YouTube,

PAY ATTENTION

Twitter, Instagram, and Facebook contain content that can skew the views of young people. They can be unduly influenced by a website, blog, or video. They can jettison their parent's beliefs, reject the values on which they were raised, and adopt beliefs that do not stand up to real scrutiny.

Some young people have, for example, bought into the idea that they can change their gender. Where did they learned that? Likely, on the internet or even from some shows that are available on Netflix or other streaming services.

As I was visiting a family, the father and his son were watching a cartoon. The father left the room and his son started watching another cartoon that looked like the 1970s show the Dukes of Hazard. This was not your father's Dukes. I watched in horror as it showed scenes of people being ejected from the car. Others were run over multiple times, and one was decapitated. Foul language was being used.

It seemed like an adult cartoon, but the son was just laughing up a storm. Had his dad been around he never would have let his son watch such violence.

Parents also need to pay attention to what they tell their children. I remember another Fourth of July celebration in which a number of families were gathered. One father was in charge of lighting the fireworks for the children. He announced that this was the last firework to be fired off.

PAY ATTENTION TO YOUR FAMILY

After that was completed, the father's son talked him into firing off many more fireworks (which were supposed to be saved for the next day). The dad said, "three more and we're done."

Two dozen more later the son said, "Let's do three more." The dad relented, and he ended up firing off all of the fireworks that were left.

This story is typical of many parents who don't hold to their word or follow through with their promises. This can be especially challenging in divorce situations, which was the case in the story above. Children quickly learn that their parents really don't mean what they say and that they can be easily manipulated.

Parents who pay attention to what they say to their children and either hold fast to what they have said, or follow through with the promises that were made, find that children have much more respect for the parents and are much more willing to obey and trust that what their parents say will be the way it is.

Spouses are not always the best at paying attention to their significant other's needs. It is easy for a husband to become so self-absorbed in his work or projects around the house that he doesn't pay attention to his wife's needs.

Under the auspices of providing for his family, the husband can neglect the wife and the rest of the family. The

PAY ATTENTION

wife could be crying out for attention, but the husband is blissfully unaware of her needs. The wife may seek attention elsewhere through another man or through throwing herself excessively into activities outside the home.

The wife can be equally as unaware of her husband's needs. After a long day at work, the husband may need to decompress before entering into the problems in the home with the children, or things that need to be done. The wife who pays attention to this need will allow the husband to be more responsive after this time of calming down from the day. These days the roles can be reversed, but the principles still apply.

Sometimes, the husband is given his space after work by the wife, but he never comes out of his so-called man cave to interact with the wife and children. This is part of the husband's failure to pay attention to his family's needs. The wife, for example, who has been home all day with the kids and has had no adult contact may be longing for some communication with her husband. She may also be looking for a respite from the parenting she has been doing all day. The aware husband can be a great boost to the wife's emotional and physical health by looking for ways to take the burden off of his wife.

I know of one wife who, as soon as her husband walked in the door, said "I'm done with the kids. They are

PAY ATTENTION TO YOUR FAMILY

all yours." She headed off to her bedroom, never to be seen for the rest of the night.

Perhaps the missing ingredient in relationships like this is honor. When we honor someone, we put their needs before ours. We seek their greatest good before seeking our own.

Paul says this in Romans 12:10 "Be devoted to one another in love. Honor one another above yourselves." Honor is a part of loving one another. "Husbands love your wives, just as Christ loved the church and gave himself up for her" (Ephesians 5:25). "In this same way, husbands ought to love their wives as their own bodies. He who loves his wife loves himself" (Ephesians 5:28).

While Paul does not say wives are to love their husbands, Jesus tells us to love one another. That should suffice. Paul does say in Ephesians 5:21 "Submit to one another out of reverence for Christ." To submit means to put the needs of others ahead of our own needs. He goes on to reinforce this when he says in the next verse, "Wives, submit yourselves to your own husbands as you do to the Lord" (Ephesians 5:22).

If husbands and wives are to submit to one another, then it seems that wives would not be called to be subservient to their husbands, but rather to honor them by seeking the greatest good for her spouse and vice-versa.

PAY ATTENTION

When it comes to **marriage**, this complementary order gives us a living illustration of the gospel message: Jesus' love for His bride, the church. Paul distinctly and clearly says that the way a man leads and cares for his wife should be a demonstration of how Jesus leads and cares for His church (Ephesians 5:25–28), and that the wife is to be submissive to his God-given leadership as she would be to Christ Himself (Ephesians 5:24). In saying this, Paul is telling us that our marriages are to be gospel plays, dramatizing how Jesus loves His church and how His church responds to His love. We are also taught that men are to lead their wives and children in loving, understanding, and compassionate ways (1 Peter 3:7).

From the first pages of the Scriptures, on through the New Testament, there is clear indication that God designed men to be the primary leaders in their families and their church communities. I don't believe that male roles of authority or leadership are only culturally determined. Neither do I believe that this design is an outgrowth of the fall of humankind. I believe the Scriptures clearly teach that God decided and determined these things when He created men and women uniquely different. That doesn't mean that men have the right to be bossy, bullying, or abusive to women in any way. And it doesn't mean that women are second class in any way. It simply means that men and

PAY ATTENTION TO YOUR FAMILY

women are designed by their Creator to be different and are therefore intended by Him to carry out differing functions in marriage and the church, roles that complement each other.

If a husband is truly loving to his wife, he will seek to honor her by treating her with all of the dignity, worth, and respect that he would show to Jesus. If a wife is truly loving to her husband, she will do the same.

When husbands and wives work together as a team, the whole family benefits. The church also benefits as the body of Christ sees the husband and wife modeling the love of Jesus towards each another.

This can only happen as we pay attention to our families.

PAY ATTENTION TO YOUR CHURCH

Are you a Christian? Are you a follower of Jesus Christ? Then you need to pay attention to your church (the local congregation) and to *the church* (Christians beyond the local gathering).

Many Christians simply look at church as a place to go on Sundays (when they feel like it). They look at church as a way to honor God one day a week. Some view church as a place where they can find comfort, peace and a break from the hectic pace of the past week.

Might I suggest that the church is not just a *place* to go on Sundays (or also perhaps during the week)? The church was originally viewed not as a building where the Christian goes, but rather as the people of God.

The church is described in the Bible as the body of Christ. The phrase "the body of Christ" is a common New Testament metaphor for the church (all those who are truly saved). The church is called "one body in Christ" in Romans 12:4–5. "For just as each of us has one body with many members, and these members do not all have the same function, so in Christ we, though many, form one body, and each member belongs to all the others."

PAY ATTENTION

Paul writes in 1 Corinthians 12:27: "Now you are the body of Christ, and each one of you is a part of it." And in Ephesians,

> So Christ himself gave the apostles, the prophets, the evangelists, the pastors and teachers, to equip his people for works of service, so that the body of Christ may be built up until we all reach unity in the faith and in the knowledge of the Son of God and become mature, attaining to the whole measure of the fullness of Christ.
> **Ephesians 4:12**

The church is clearly equated with "the body" of Christ in Ephesians 5:23: "For the husband is the head of the wife as Christ is the head of the church, his body, of which he is the Savior."

Colossians 1:24 further reinforces this idea when Paul says, "Now I rejoice in what I am suffering for you, and I fill up in my flesh what is still lacking in regard to Christ's afflictions, for the sake of his body, which is the church."

When we talk about the church we are talking about the body of Christ, the Christian people of God. We can go to a church building to worship with or meet with *the church.*

Paying attention to this one detail will keep us from thinking that the church is a place rather than our brothers and sisters in Christ. We come to realize that *the church* is people.

In the 1973 movie Soylent Green, moviegoers were shocked by one of the last lines in the movie when the main character, Thorn boards a truck transporting bodies from the euthanasia center to a recycling plant, where the secret is revealed: human corpses are being converted into Soylent Green (food for the population to eat). Thorn is wounded and as he is being taken to the hospital he shouts to all "Soylent Green is people!"

We can shout out "*the church* is people."

When St. Paul describes the church as the body of Christ, he is using this image to show that the people of God are all a part of Christ's body. We are a part of His body in the sense that as some have said, "we are the hands, feet and voice of Christ" on this earth.

This means that each Christian is an important part of the body of Christ. Paul says in 1 Corinthians 12:12 and following that each Christian has a role to play in the functioning of the body of Christ. Each person is vital to help the body operate as it should.

Paul emphasizes this when he writes,

> Just as a body, though one, has many parts, but all its many parts form one body, so it is with Christ. For we were all baptized by one

PAY ATTENTION

Spirit so as to form one body—whether Jews or Gentiles, slave or free—and we were all given the one Spirit to drink. Even so the body is not made up of one part but of many. Now if the foot should say, "Because I am not a hand, I do not belong to the body," it would not for that reason stop being part of the body. And if the ear should say, "Because I am not an eye, I do not belong to the body," it would not for that reason stop being part of the body. If the whole body were an eye, where would the sense of hearing be? If the whole body were an ear, where would the sense of smell be? But in fact, God has placed the parts in the body, every one of them, just as he wanted them to be. If they were all one part, where would the body be? As it is, there are many parts, but one body. The eye cannot say to the hand, "I don't need you!" And the head cannot say to the feet, "I don't need you!" On the contrary, those parts of the body that seem to be weaker are indispensable, and the parts that we think are less honorable we treat with special honor. And the parts that are unpresentable are treated with special modesty, while our presentable parts need no special treatment. But God has put the body together, giving greater honor to the parts that lacked it, so that there should be no division in the body, but that its parts should have equal concern for each other. If one part suffers, every part suffers with it; if one part is honored, every part rejoices with it. Now you

PAY ATTENTION TO YOUR CHURCH

> are the body of Christ, and each one of you is a part of it.
>
> **1 Corinthians 12:12–27**

There are people in the church that have obvious gifts and talents. Paul speaks about this,

> And God has placed in the church first of all apostles, second prophets, third teachers, then miracles, then gifts of healing, of helping, of guidance, and of different kinds of tongues. Are all apostles? Are all prophets? Are all teachers? Do all work miracles? Do all have gifts of healing? Do all speak in tongues? Do all interpret? Now eagerly desire the greater gifts.
>
> **1 Corinthians 12:28**

These are just some of the supernatural spiritual gifts listed in the New Testament. That doesn't even include the Spirit inspired natural talents and abilities that Christians have.

The Old Testament describes how God has given certain people the ability to do creative things. In Exodus 35 we read:

> Then Moses said to the Israelites, "See, the LORD has chosen Bezalel son of Uri, the son of Hur, of the tribe of Judah, and he has filled him with the Spirit of God, with wisdom, with understanding, with knowledge and with all kinds of skills—to make artistic designs for work in

PAY ATTENTION

> gold, silver and bronze, to cut and set stones, to work in wood and to engage in all kinds of artistic crafts. And he has given both him and Oholiab son of Ahisamak, of the tribe of Dan, the ability to teach others. He has filled them with skill to do all kinds of work as engravers, designers, embroiderers in blue, purple and scarlet yarn and fine linen, and weavers—all of them skilled workers and designers."
>
> **Exodus 35:30–35**

There is a man in my church that is a contractor. His natural talents and abilities have served our church in many ways. He has helped in certain construction projects, he has repaired many things in the church facilities, and most importantly given us wise advice when we had questions about things related to our buildings. He has used these talents and abilities for the glory of God and the benefit of the church.

A former urologist in our parish also has a gift of painting. He has created some beautiful and inspiring paintings. He even painted a portrait of me which was amazing (although I doubt a portrait of this author would inspire anyone).

The promise is that the Holy Spirit will give spiritual gifts to all Christians. All these (gifts) are the work of one and the same Spirit, and He distributes them to each one, just as He determines (1 Corinthians 12:11).

PAY ATTENTION TO YOUR CHURCH

This means that everyone in the body of Christ is important to the church. Each person has a role to play, gifts to use, talents to share. Each person also matters to the church. There are some in the church with high profile ministries. Others serve in ministries that are not as glamorous. Still others have what may seem to them as insignificant roles to play in the church.

There are a couple of women in my church who have a ministry that no one else seems to want. They routinely clean up the kitchen, putting away dishes that others have put in the dishwasher or in the drainer, cleaning out the refrigerator of left over or outdated food, and organizing the kitchen cupboards so that items are easy to find. This "Martha ministry" often causes them on occasion to posit that others should be doing this. "I'm not their mother! They should know how to put things away." However, these women do this because they love the Lord and love the church. I might add, they pay attention to the kitchen. This is just one example of members going beyond the norm for the benefit of the other members of the body of Christ.

It is important for each member of the church to find their particular role or ministry. The ideal is to take on a role or ministry for which you have a passion. Often, that passion can be an indication of the gifting that God has

PAY ATTENTION

given you for that particular function in the body of Christ. That ministry can be within the walls of the church building or outside of it.

Our church did not have a grief support or recovery group until one of our members' husband died. She did not know where to turn for help and support. She began to do research on how to deal with grief. She came across some resources that helped her. She was inspired to start a grief support group in our church. The group, called Shadowlands (after C.S. Lewis' description of the grief he went through when his wife died), met for many years and has been a help to both members of our church and others outside of the church.

One of my daughters, Alexandra, used to lead a small group of Christians that met at the home of one of the group members. She has a real gift for leading young people to focus on biblical study, love, and service. The members of her group knew that she is paying attention to them.

Another area of the church life to which we need to pay attention is in the area of finances. Some have the idea that the church is always asking for money. Granted, there have been churches for which that seems to be true, but the reality is that in order to function as a church in a particular location, finances are needed.

We don't think twice when our children come home

PAY ATTENTION TO YOUR CHURCH

from school asking for money for a uniform, piece of equipment, supplies, or field trip. We don't stop going to the doctor because they charge a co-pay or require extra payments for some services.

When it comes to the church, some people don't understand what it takes to run a church. From mortgages, to utilities, to repairs, to upgrades, the day-to-day expenses of the church can be very high. Then you have salaries of staff members, diocesan assessments, and insurance payments; all of which add to the expense of running a church.

Most church members want the church to do things like offer services, ministries, continuing education for adults and children, and to reach out to the community. Each of these things cost money.

The problem is that many have the idea that it is the job of the rich or well-off to support the church. A person I know prided themselves in being a generous tipper at restaurants. This person thought nothing of leaving a $20 or more tip for a server, but when the offering plate was passed around, this person thought he was being generous in putting a five-dollar bill into the plate.

> A priest, minister, and rabbi are talking about how they offer up the take from the collection plate to God. Well, says the priest, I draw a line on the floor, throw all the money into the air, and everything that lands on one side I keep,

> everything that lands on the other I give to God. Not bad says the minister. I draw a circle on the ground, throw all the money into the air, and whatever lands inside the circle I keep and whatever lands outside the circle I give to God. I do something similar, says the rabbi. I take all the money, throw it into the air, and what God catches, he can keep. (Welby, 2003).

There are many generous pastors, priests, and rabbis, and some that are not so much. This story is not just about the clergy, it is about how most people approach their giving to God.

Some of the most generous people in the church are widows who do not have all that much to give. Much like the poor widow in Mark 12:41–44, whom Jesus commended for her giving, many widows in churches give much more than even some of the more well-off members.

When we pay attention to our giving to the church, we can often be inspired by Scripture to give with the right attitude. As we pay attention to our relationship with Jesus, He can speak to us about what we are to give for the work of His kingdom.

> A mother wanted to teach her daughter a moral lesson. She gave the little girl a quarter and a dollar for church. "Put whichever one you want in the collection plate and keep the other for

yourself," she told the girl. When they were coming out of church, the mother asked her daughter which amount she had given. "Well," said the little girl, "I was going to give the dollar, but just before the collection the man in the pulpit said that we should all be cheerful givers. I knew I'd be a lot more cheerful if I gave the quarter, so I did." (Bits & Pieces, 1993, 23).

The brilliant comedian and movie actor W.C. Fields led an unrestrained showbiz life displaying a fondness for alcohol and mistresses. He was not known as a religious man, but as his death approached he began to read the Bible. When a friend asked him about this behavior he humorously explained that he was: Looking for loopholes. (Quote Investigator, 2016)

Unfortunately, some Christians are looking for loopholes when it comes to giving to God through His church. One such loophole is to say that Jesus did away with the Old Testament command to tithe (to give a tenth of one's income).

While some may argue that New Testament Christians are not required to tithe. May I suggest that Jesus believed in tithing? Pay attention to what He says in Matthew:

> Woe to you, teachers of the law and Pharisees, you hypocrites! You give a tenth [a tithe] of your spices—mint, dill and cumin. But you

PAY ATTENTION

have neglected the more important matters of the law—justice, mercy and faithfulness. You should have practiced the latter, without neglecting the former.

Matthew 23:23–24

Notice what Jesus says here. "You give a tenth, a tithe as the Law of Moses requires, but you have neglected doing justly, loving mercy and walking faithfully with your God" (see Micah 6:8). Then He said, "you should have practiced the latter without neglecting the former [tithing]."

Jesus knew full well what the Old Testament says about tithing. He would have been familiar with the passage in Malachi 3

> "I the Lord do not change. So you, the descendants of Jacob, are not destroyed. Ever since the time of your ancestors you have turned away from my decrees and have not kept them. Return to me, and I will return to you," says the Lord Almighty. "But you ask, 'How are we to return?' 'Will a mere mortal rob God? Yet you rob me.'" "But you ask, 'How are we robbing you?' "In tithes and offerings. You are under a curse—your whole nation—because you are robbing me. Bring the whole tithe into the storehouse, that there may be food in my house. Test me in this,' says the Lord Almighty, 'and see if I will not throw open the floodgates

PAY ATTENTION TO YOUR CHURCH

of heaven and pour out so much blessing that there will not be room enough to store it.'"

Malachi 3:6–10

The promise of God is that as they practice tithing (as a way of showing their dependence upon God's provision), they will not be robbing God. After all, it was God who gives them the ability to have the resources they have (Deuteronomy 8:18).

Notice also, that in Malachi, God speaks of tithes and offerings. Offerings are gifts given above and beyond a tithe. In the church, Christians often give a tithe of their income, but they also occasionally give beyond their tithe to meet other needs. For example, our denomination has what is called, the Anglican Relief and Development Fund. This fund helps meet needs all over the world. Our church members occasionally feel led to give an extra gift or offering to this fund.

If, as Paul says in 1 Corinthians 10:26, "the earth is the Lord's and everything in it," then everything belongs to God. God allows us to have and acquire the finances we have and allows us to keep 90 percent and asks us to give 10 percent. It is from this 90 percent that Christians often feel moved by the Spirit to give an extra offering.

Notice that the tithe is to be brought into the storehouse. Today, we understand the storehouse to mean the church. As we bring our tithes into the church, we will not only allow the work of the kingdom of God to go on but will also be able to make a difference in the lives of those inside and outside of the church not only for time, but also for eternity.

Could it be that by following God's direction in giving that we might indeed "open the floodgates of heaven" and receive such a blessing that we might not have room enough to store it?

This seems to indicate that there is a law of reciprocity at work here. Jesus said in Luke 6:38: "Give, and it will be given to you. A good measure, pressed down, shaken together, and running over will be poured into your lap. For with the measure you use, it will be measured back to you."

Christians often base their giving on what they have rather than on what God would want them to give. St. Paul gives us an example of giving that is not based upon what one has, but rather on one's attitude towards giving.

In 2 Corinthians, Paul talks about the Macedonian Christians and their generosity.

> Now, brothers, we want you to know about the grace that God has given the churches of Macedonia. In the terrible ordeal they suffered, their abundant joy and deep poverty overflowed into rich generosity. For I testify that they gave according to their ability and even beyond it. Of

their own accord, they earnestly pleaded with us for the privilege of sharing in this service to the saints. And not only did they do as we expected, but they gave themselves first to the Lord and then to us, because it was the will of God.

2 Corinthians 8:1–5 (BSB)

Notice, the Macedonians gave because of a generous spirit they had within them. They were suffering under a great ordeal causing them to have a deep poverty. In spite of this, their abundant joy within them overflowed with rich generosity. So much so, that they entirely on their own, without pressure or a guilt trip being laid on them, they pleaded with Paul for the privilege of helping the Jerusalem Christians, who were themselves financially hanging on by a thread. We get the sense that these Jerusalem Christians were even worse off than were the Macedonian Christians.

But they didn't just give money, it says they first gave themselves to the Lord, then to the apostles by their financial gift. Giving by itself is a good thing, but true Christian giving is done by the believer giving themselves fully to the Lord first. By so doing, the Christian can be open to the leading of Jesus by the Holy Spirit to be inspired to give and to be directed as to how much to give.

Paul goes on to teach in 2 Corinthians,

PAY ATTENTION

> Remember this: Whoever sows sparingly will also reap sparingly, and whoever sows generously will also reap generously. Each one should give what he has decided in his heart to give, not out of regret or compulsion. For God loves a cheerful giver. And God is able to make all grace abound to you, so that in all things, at all times, having all that you need, you will abound in every good work.
> **2 Corinthians 9:6–8**

The idea of sowing here is that as we use the financial resources God has given us as He directs us, our giving is like planting a seed which can sprout into something greater. As we give generously, we will also reap generously. As we give with a desire to make a difference in the life of an individual, family, community, church or the world, we will receive blessings in return. This doesn't always mean we will receive financial blessings in return. The blessings we receive may be spiritual in nature, but the promise is that we will receive blessings in return for our giving.

This is dependent upon the attitude with which we give. Each person should decide for himself what he has determined (by the help of the Holy Spirit) to give. Giving should not be done out of guilt or regret for something bad we have done. Nor should our giving be done to try to earn God's love or forgiveness. We should not give because the pastor lays a guilt trip upon us or by the use of some manipulation to compel us to give.

PAY ATTENTION TO YOUR CHURCH

When we give with the right attitude, we are giving as God wants us to give. Why? Because God loves a cheerful giver. That word cheerful in the Greek language is the word from which we get the word hilarious. So, God, loves a hilarious giver.

I can't say that I have seen that type of joy many times when the offering plate is passed. I have seen the joyful giver often in the generosity with which they give.

When we give with this hilarious attitude, Paul says God is able to make all grace abound to you. Sometimes that grace will be in the form of a return of financial blessing to you. As a result, the cheerful giver who sows generously will not only have all that they need to live on but will have even more to give back to the work of the Lord and/or to help others in need. They will abound in every good work.

This law of reciprocity or promise of blessing from God is for a purpose. That purpose is not just so that we will get rich, but rather that we will have more with which to bless others. We don't give to God in order to get something for ourselves, but when we do give with the right spirit, we will receive blessings from God so that we can make a difference in the lives of others.

We don't necessarily need to wait for those blessings in order to give. Remember, the Macedonians gave out of

PAY ATTENTION

their extreme poverty, and they gave joyfully as they determined in their heart what God wanted them to give.

One of the problems that keeps Christians from giving generously (or at all) is the large amount of debt that families and individuals have. From student debt, to mortgages, to car payments, to credit card debt, etc., the pressure is on the average Christian to try to figure out how to survive without declaring bankruptcy or worse.

Many Christians have never learned how to budget, control their spending, delay gratification, and even save for the future. We are enslaved by the people and institutions to which we are indebted.

In Romans 13:7 Paul reminds us to,

> Give to everyone what you owe them: If you owe taxes, pay taxes; if revenue, then revenue; if respect, then respect; if honor, then honor. Let no debt remain outstanding, except the continuing debt to love one another, for whoever loves others has fulfilled the law.
> **Romans 13:7**

Imagine the freedom you would feel if you didn't owe anything to anyone. Obviously, there may be some debt that could be necessary (i.e. a mortgage), but many have made it their goal to get out of all debt as quickly as they can. This often requires sacrifice, doing without some things, cutting back on others, and implementing cost reducing efforts.

Author Dave Ramsey, in his *Total Money Makeover*, gives practical suggestions on how one can get out of debt and "live like no one else, so that you can live like no one else." (Ramsey, 2003). His guiding principle is that the more debt you can get rid of, the more finances you have to do some of the things you want to do and also to help out and be a blessing to your church and to those in need.

What Ramsey would say is that whether one has much or little, our attitude towards God is most important. In the book of Proverbs, we read the prayer of Agur.

> Give me neither poverty nor riches but give me only my daily bread. Otherwise, I may have too much and disown you and say, "Who is the Lord?" or I may become poor and steal and dishonor the name of my God.
>
> **Proverbs 30:8–9**

Indeed, that is the danger; the rich could become arrogant and forget the Lord, and think they can take care of themselves.

Does that mean it is wrong to be rich, or that wealth is an evil? While Jesus did say that it is difficult for the rich to get into heaven (Mark 10:17–27), it can't be wrong to have riches for the Lord Himself makes people rich. He made Abraham rich, and Isaac, and the people of Israel in the Promised Land.

PAY ATTENTION

> When the LORD your God brings you into the land he swore to your fathers, to Abraham, Isaac and Jacob, to give you—a land with large, flourishing cities you did not build, houses filled with all kinds of good things you did not provide, wells you did not dig, and vineyards and olive groves you did not plant—then when you eat and are satisfied, be careful that you do not forget the LORD, who brought you out of Egypt, out of the land of slavery.
>
> **Deuteronomy 6:10–12**

The problem is not the riches they would have, but the temptation to forget the God who made it all possible. The New Testament as well tells us we shouldn't only focus on the spiritual blessings that come to us from the heavenly realms. Today, the fruits of the field, the prosperity in the land, and the wealth of the nations, are blessings of God. Wealth and riches are not necessarily a curse.

St. Paul says this to the Christians under Timothy's leadership.

> Command those who are rich in this present world not to be arrogant nor to put their hope in wealth, which is so uncertain, but to put their hope in God, who richly provides us with everything for our enjoyment. Command them to do good, to be rich in good deeds, and to be generous and willing to share. In this way they will lay up treasure for themselves as a firm

PAY ATTENTION TO YOUR CHURCH

foundation for the coming age, so that they may take hold of the life that is truly life.

1 Timothy 6:17–19

Notice that Paul does not say that Christians shouldn't have riches, but that they should not forget God "who richly provides us with everything for our enjoyment." One of the blessings of God is that we can enjoy life. God doesn't begrudge us having money, possessions, going on trips, and saving for the future. What God is concerned about is that we don't forget Him or that we don't forget those in need.

As we are good stewards of what God has given us, we are laying up treasures for ourselves as a firm foundation for the coming age. Our gifts and our giving can't earn our way into heaven, nor do they mean we deserve new life with God. Heaven and new life are possible only by faith in Christ, who gives it by grace. But what rich prospects we have when we use God's gifts and blessings in thankfulness and love to Him, being rich in good deeds and being generous in our sharing.

Paul is saying, "God richly provides us with everything for our enjoyment, to do good, to be rich in good deeds, and to be generous and willing to share."

What happens, however, is that people make prosperity a curse. That's what happens when people live for wealth and riches and trust in them. When people's attitude shows, "I am rich, I don't need the Lord; I can look after myself." Or when people say, "I am rich, and I better make sure that I stay rich, for my hope and happiness depend on these things." That is a danger not just for millionaires, but for all of us. That danger is in the heart of all of us.

You often hear the misquotation of the Bible when people say, "The Bible says that money is the root of all evil." Actually, Paul says in 1 Timothy 6:10: "For the love of money is a root of all kinds of evil. Some people, eager for money, have wandered from the faith and pierced themselves with many griefs."

So, money is not the root of all evil, but the love of money. When money becomes a god for a person, they are prone to all kinds of evil.

Perhaps there is great wisdom in the words of the writer to the Hebrews:

> Keep your lives free from the love of money and be content with what you have, because God has said, "Never will I leave you; never will I forsake you." So, we say with confidence, "The Lord is my helper; I will not be afraid. What can mere mortals do to me?
> **Hebrews 13:5–6**

As we pay attention to our church and our giving, God's kingdom, God's world, and we can be blessed.

CONCLUSION

It is important that we pay attention to our bodies, minds, and spirits.

It is equally important to pay attention to what God's Word written says. As we get into the Word of God and get the Word of God into us we will be drawn closer to the way of God, the truth of God and the life of God. We will be drawn closer to Jesus.

In fact, Jesus said, "You study the Scriptures diligently because you think that in them you have eternal life. These are the very Scriptures that testify about me, yet you refuse to come to me to have life" (John 5:39–40).

I believe God is speaking to each reader through this book. If you have not yet turned your life over to Jesus by asking Him to be your Savior and seeking to follow Him as your Lord (ruler) then you would want to first confess your sins to God, agree to turn away from them (repentance), then invite Jesus to come into your life, forgive you and give you a new life. When you ask Him into your life, He will send His Holy Spirit as His representative. The Holy Spirit will begin to change your life for the better. Ask Jesus to fill you with the Holy Spirit so that you will have God's power to live the sort of life God wants for you.

PAY ATTENTION

Perhaps God is not speaking to you with every word or on every page. But whenever God is speaking to you, pay attention. "Listen and hear my voice; pay attention and hear what I say" (Isaiah 28:23).

ABOUT THE AUTHOR

The Very Reverend Dr. Roger Grist was born in Dallas, Texas. He graduated from high school in Dallas. He received a bachelor of arts degree in journalism from Texas Tech University. He received a master of divinity from Melodyland School of Theology. He received a Doctor of Ministry degree from Bakke Graduate University.

His doctoral dissertation is entitled *Biblical Interpretation and the Episcopal Church: A Proposal for a Return to a Conservative Hermeneutic.*

Father Grist, as he is known in his church circles, has served churches in Bakersfield, CA, Centralia, WA, Portland, OR, Buffalo, NY, and most recently Fort Worth, TX, where he is the Rector/Pastor of St. Anne's Anglican Church. He has served this congregation for nineteen years.

He is married to his wife of thirty-eight years, Nancy Grist. They have two daughters, Alexandra and Elizabeth.

BIBLIOGRAPHY

Anglican Church in North American. *The Book of Common Prayer*. Huntington Beach, CA: Anglican Liturgy Press, 2019.

Bits & Pieces. "Cheerful Givers." February 4, 1993.

Brendyn. "Stiff Neck Word of Knowledge Leads to Restored Mobility." *Trip Testimonies. Global Awakening*. December, nd., 2019. https://globalawakening.com/trips/trip-testimonies/brazil-december-2019/stiff-neck-word-of-knowledge-leads-to-restored-mobility

Brumback, Carl. *What Meaneth This*. Springfield, MO: Gospel Publishing House, 1947. Google groups. "No fish." January 29, 2000. https://groups.google.com/g/alt.tasteless.jokes/c/n8w6qX9Oma0/m/sqQ16p2cUMoJ

Irenaeus. *Against Heresies*. Jackson, MI: Ex Fontibus Company, 1981.

Johnson, Bill and Randy Clark. *The Essential Guide to Healing*. Bloomington, MN: Chosen Books, 2011.

Kendrick, Klaude. *The Promise Fulfilled*. Springfield, MO: Gospel Publishing House, 1961.

Lusk, Teresa. "How to Activate the Gift of the Word of Knowledge." *Teresa Lusk Ministries*. October 27, 2020. https://www.teresalusk.com/post/how-to-activate-the-gift-of-the-word-of-knowledge.

PAY ATTENTION

Mackie, Alexander. *The Gift of Tongues*. New York: Doubleday and Company, 1950.

McGuire, Barry. 1975. "I Walked a Mile." Track 10 on *To the Bride*. Myrrh Records, compact disc.

Minnix, J. Mike. "The Congregation that Gave Too Much." *PastorLife.com*. n.d. https://www.pastorlife.com/members/sermon.asp?SERMON_ID=7146&fm=author-bio&authorid=1

Quote Investigator. "I'm Looking for Loopholes." May 8, 2016. https://quoteinvestigator.com/2016/05/08/loopholes/

Ramsey, Dave. *Total Money Makeover*. Nashville, TN: Thomas Nelson, 2003.

Sherril, John. *They Speak with Other Tongues*. Westwood, NJ: Revell Company, 1964.

Short, Brian. "Classroom Classic." *Allnurses*.com. February 27, 2002. https://allnurses.com/classroom-classic-t13252/.

Stick With Jesus. "It SOUNDS Like a Squirrel…!" January 27, 2017. https://stickwithjesus.wordpress.com/2017/01/27/it-sounds-like-a-squirrel/.

Welby. April, 2003. "A Priest, a Minister, and a Rabbi." *Straight Dope Message Board* (Message board). *The Straight Dope*. April, 2003. https://boards.straightdope.com/t/a-priest-a-minister-and-a-rabbi/169040/6

BIBLIOGRAPHY

Taylor, Katherine. "No easy way." *News24*. March 1, 2014. https://www.news24.com/you/archive/no-easy-way-20170728.

Tertullian. *The Anti Nicene Fathers,* New York: Charles Scribner's 1885.

Wimber, John and Kevin Springer. *Power Evangelism*. Bloomington, MN: Chosen Books, 2009. The Episcopal Church. *The Book of Common Prayer ad Administration of the Sacraments ad other Rites and Ceremovies of the Church*. New York: Church Publishing Incorporated, 2007.

Zeolla, Gary F. "Dead Men Do Bleed!" *Darkness to Light Ministry newsletter*. April, 1997. https://www.zeolla.org/christian/apologetics/article/dead-men.htm.

CPSIA information can be obtained
at www.ICGtesting.com
Printed in the USA
BVHW052238090623
665714BV00005B/85